Coastal Wetland Trends in the Narragansett Bay Estuary During the 20th Century

November 2004

A National Wetlands Inventory Cooperative Interagency Report

Coastal Wetland Trends in the Narragansett Bay Estuary During the 20th Century

Ralph W. Tiner[1], Irene J. Huber[2], Todd Nuerminger[2], and Aimée L. Mandeville[3]

[1]U.S. Fish & Wildlife Service
National Wetlands Inventory Program
Northeast Region
300 Westgate Center Drive
Hadley, MA 01035

[2]Natural Resources Assessment Group
Department of Plant and Soil Sciences
University of Massachusetts
Stockbridge Hall
Amherst, MA 01003

[3]Department of Natural Resources Science
Environmental Data Center
University of Rhode Island
1 Greenhouse Road, Room 105
Kingston, RI 02881

November 2004

National Wetlands Inventory Cooperative Interagency Report between
U.S. Fish & Wildlife Service, University of Massachusetts-Amherst, University of Rhode Island, and Rhode Island Department of Environmental Management

Table of Contents

List of Tables

List of Tables (continued)

List of Figures

Introduction

The Rhode Island Department of Environmental Management's Narragansett Bay Estuary Program's (NBEP) goal is to protect and preserve Narragansett Bay through conserving and restoring natural resources and enhancing water quality. NBEP accomplishes this through a variety of projects, including interagency partnerships and community involvement. To manage these valuable resources, NBEP wanted baseline information on coastal wetlands and their buffers. With the aid of the University of Massachusett (UMass), University of Rhode Island (URI), and the U.S. Fish and Wildlife Service (FWS), NBEP obtained an inventory of current coastal wetlands, the 500-foot buffer zone, and potential wetland restoration sites for the estuary. While knowing the current state of these resources is vital to managing the resource, an analysis of trends in these resources would help identify threats and put the presentday resources in a historic context.

In 1999, the NBEP and the FWS modified an existing cooperative agreement to produce wetland trends information for the Narragansett Bay Estuary. The FWS works in partnership with UMass (Department of Plant and Soil Sciences, Natural Resources Assessment Group - NRAG) to conduct wetland mapping, trend analysis, and other studies requiring interpretation of aerial photography. NBEP also has an agreement with the URI to perform the geographic information system (GIS) services. URI also played a major role in this project by providing these services. The NBEP will use the results of this work to help develop a coastal wetland conservation and restoration strategy for the Narragansett Bay Estuary.

This report presents the results of this multi-agency cooperative project. It summarizes data for the entire estuary and for several pilot study areas where trends were analyzed back to the 1930s.

Study Area

The Narragansett Bay Estuary is a 147-square mile coastal embayment (including Mount Hope Bay) that dominates the Rhode Island landscape (Figures 1 and 2). It is the receiving basin for seven major watersheds in Rhode Island and Massachusetts including the Blackstone, Moshassuck, Pawtuxet, Taunton, Ten Mile, Warren, and Woonaquatucket. The Estuary is defined by the limits of brackish tidal water and hydrogeomorphology. The baywide coastal wetlands trends analysis (1950s-1990s) was limited to the Rhode Island portion. Within the Narragansett Bay Estuary, six areas were selected as pilot areas to examine wetland trends from the 1930s-1950s in addition to the 1950s-1990s analysis done baywide: 1) Allins Cove, 2) Calf Pasture Point, 3) Jacobs Point, 4) Palmer River, 5) Sachuest Point, and 6) Wesquage Pond (Figure 3).

Figure 1. Location of the Narragansett Bay Estuary and its drainage area; the general boundary of the estuary is the dark gray-shaded area.

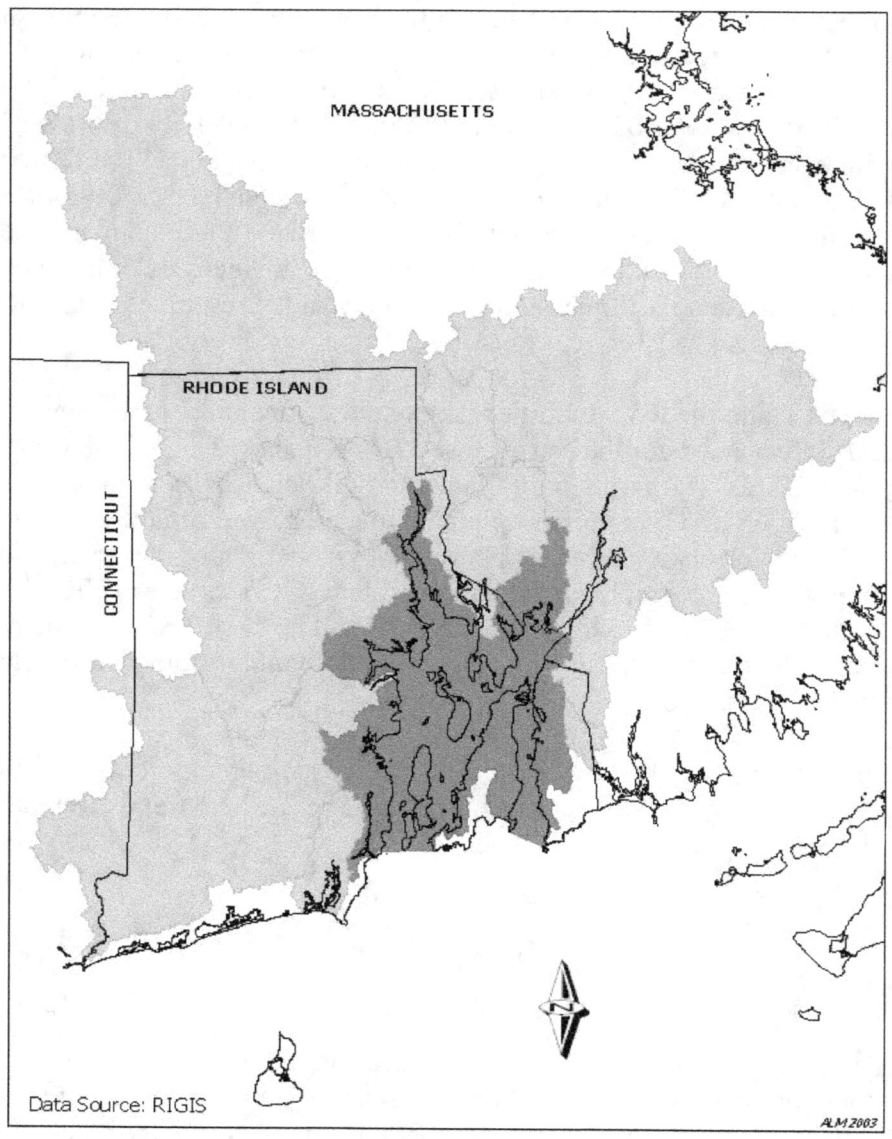

Figure 2. Limits of the Narragansett Bay Estuary as defined for this study.

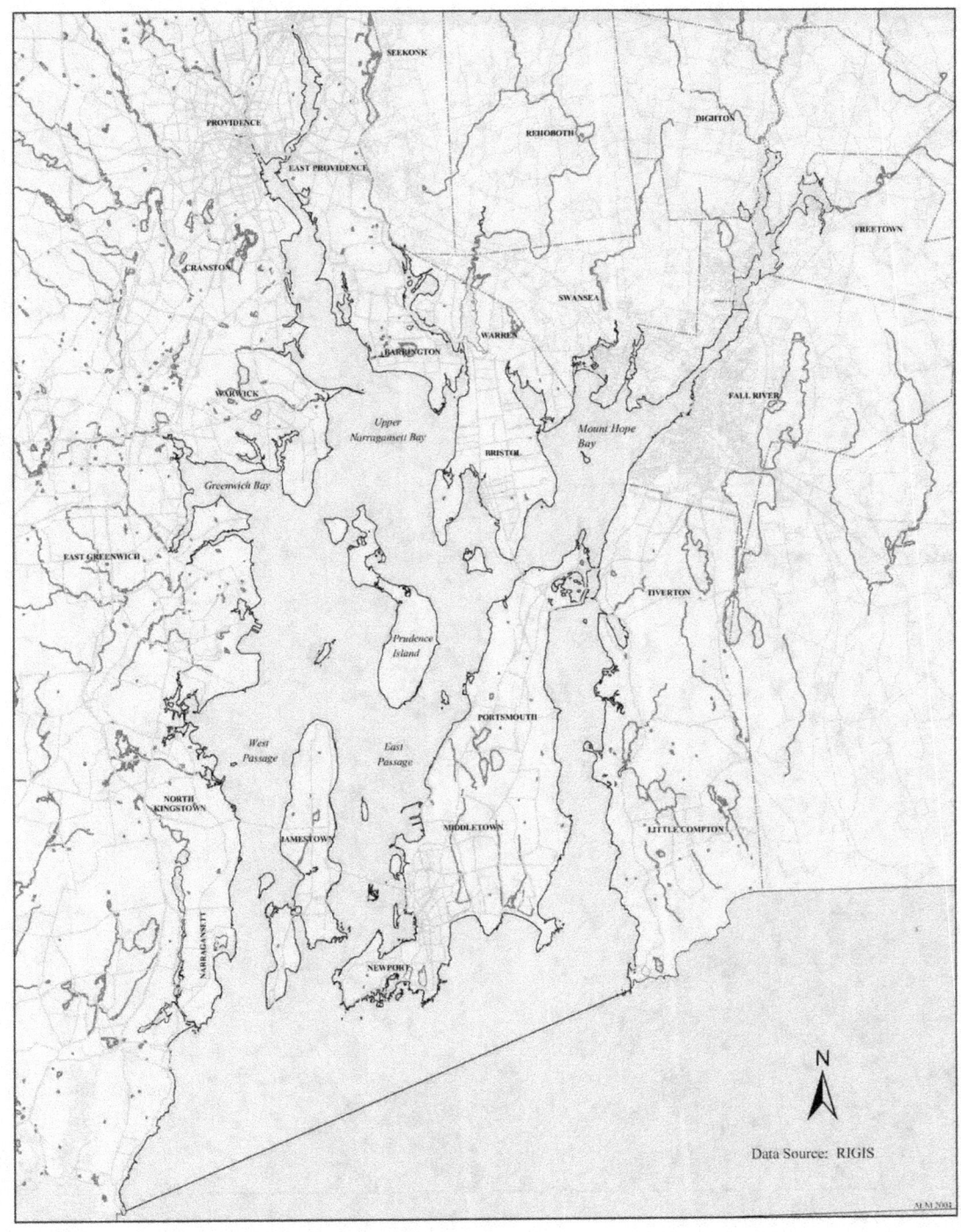

Figure 3. Location of six pilot areas within the Narragansett Bay Estuary.

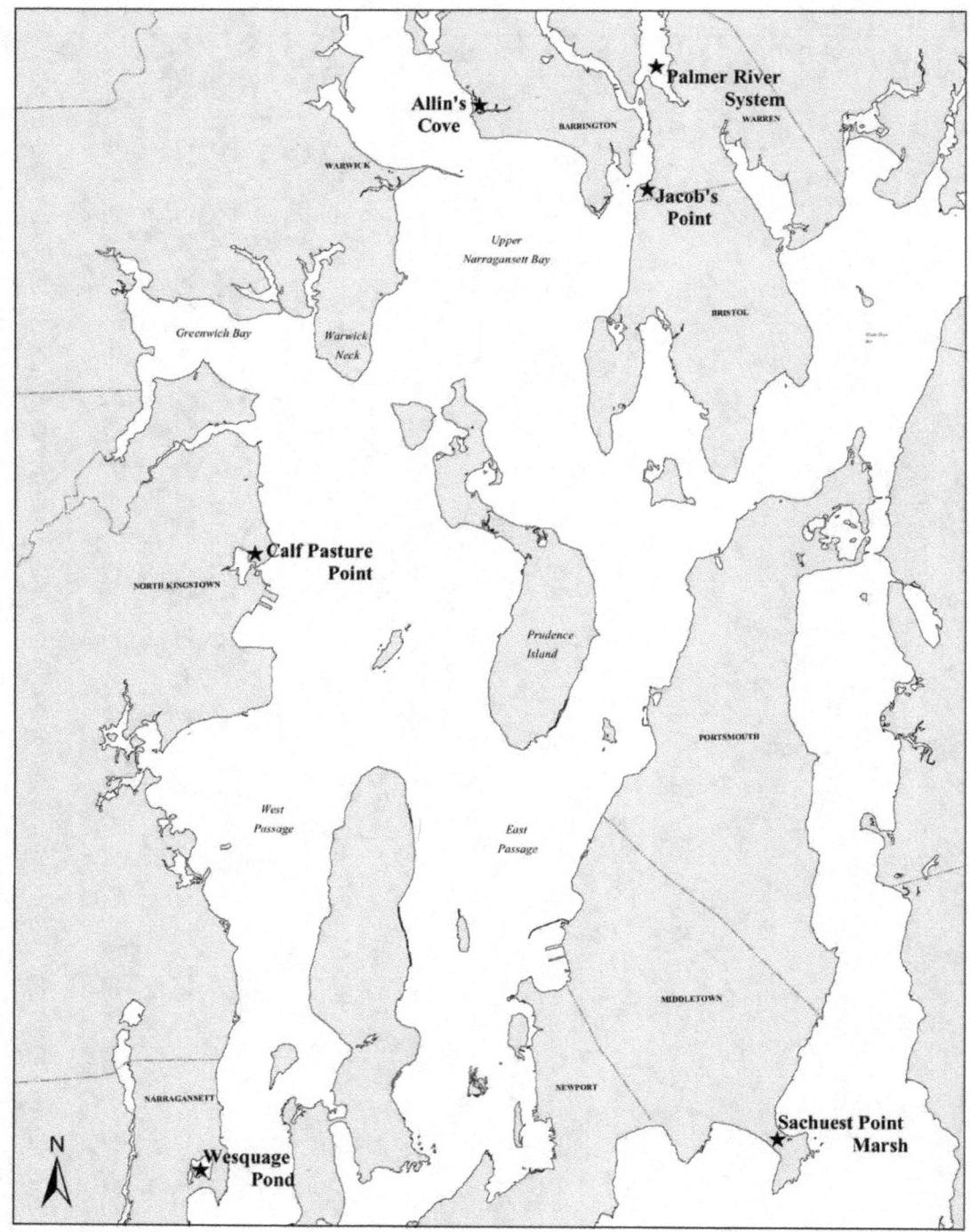

Methods

Data Compiliation

Conventional photointerpretation techniques were used to identify trends in coastal wetlands and the 500-buffer around these wetlands. For the Narragansett Bay study area, trends from the 1950s to the 1990s were determined. For the six pilot study areas (Allins Cove, Calf Pasture Point, Jacobs Point, Palmer River, Sachuset Point, and Wesquage Pond), coastal wetland trends were identified for two time periods: the late1930s/early 1940s-1950s and the 1950s-1990s. Table 1 summarizes the aerial photography used for the study.

Photointerpretation was performed using mirror stereoscopes. Wetlands and deepwater habitats were classified according to "Classification of Wetlands and Deepwater Habitats of the United States" (Cowardin et al. 1979), the national digital data standard for wetland inventory and reporting on wetland trends. For this study, coastal wetlands include Cowardin's marine and estuarine intertidal wetlands - tidal wetlands with measurable traces of ocean-derived salts. Wetland changes to and from nonwetlands were categorized according to the features presented in Table 2. These features represent modifications of the Anderson et al. (1976) national land use/cover classification system. Multiple codes may be assigned to a change in a given wetland. Wetland trends were marked on acetate overlays attached to aerial photographs. Changes in wetlands and deepwater habitats were interpreted using Bausch & Lomb stereo integration scopes. Land use/cover changes in the 500-foot buffer around coastal wetlands were identified using a Bausch & Lomb stereo zoom transfer scope (ZTS) which was also used to match photointerpreted trends data to 1:24,000 frosted mylar maps (prepared by URI). The mylar overlays showing trends were digitized for GIS analysis. The minimum mapping unit for wetland change polygons was 0.25 acre, although smaller polygons of wetland loss were mapped. For more detailed information on methods, see Huber and Nuerminger (2003).

Table 1. Aerial photography used for this study. <u>Note</u>: The 1990s photographs for pilot study areas were the same as used baywide for this period.

Study Area	Study Period	Aerial Photography Used		
		Scale	Emulsion	Date
Entire Bay	1990s	1:40,000	True Color	8/11/96
		1:12,000	True Color	7/6/96
	1950s	1:24,000	Black&White	10-11/51; 5/52
Allins Cove	1930s	1:28,000	Black&White	12/13/38
	1950s	1:20,000	Black&White	5/15/52
Calf Pasture Point	1930s	1:28,000	Black&White	12/13/38
	1950s	1:20,000	Black&White	10/26/51
Jacobs Point	1930s	1:28,000	Black&White	12/13/38
	1950s	1:20,000	Black&White	10/21/51
Palmer River	1930/40s	1:28,000	Black&White	12/13/38; 10/24/41
	1950s	1:20,000	Black&White	10/21/51
Sachuest Point	1930s	1:28,000	Black&White	12/13/38
	1950s	1:20,000	Black&White	10/21/51
Wesquage Pond	1940s	1:28,000	Black&White	10/8/41
	1950s	1:20,000	Black&White	10/26/51

Table 2. Causes of wetland losses, gains, and changes in type.

Cause	Brief Definition
Agriculture	Area subject to farming practices including cropland, orchards, nurseries, vineyards, ornamental horticulture, pasture and hayfields
Barren Land	Nonvegetated or sparsely vegetated lands including mixed, sandy areas (not beaches), strip mines, quarries, and gravel pits
Coastal Processes	Natural processes associated with tidal currents and wave action including erosion, accretion, and dune migration (overwash)
Commercial & Services	Commercial and institutional structures, marinas, paved surfaces, unpaved surfaces, recreational structures, wharves, piers, and shipyards
Ditching	Shallow linear excavation designed to improve drainage; ditches may be filled in to restore wetland hydrology
Erosion from Boat Traffic	Shoreline erosion caused by wakes generated by boats (limited to marina areas)
Excavation	Removal of earth or soil from wetlands or bay and channel bottoms
Forest	Wooded area dominated by trees (deciduous, evergreen, or mixed)
Industrial & Commercial Complexes	Development involving a mixture of factories and business establishments
Jetties & Groins	Artificial rocky structures to maintain navigable channels (jetty) or beaches (groin); these structures may be built or removed
Oyster Colonization	Establishment of an oyster reef
Rangeland	Old fields and thickets (herbaceous, shrub and brush, or mixed cover)
Residential Development	Houses and apartments including lawns
Soil Deposition	Fill material from upland sources deposited in wetlands or waters
Spoil Deposition	Dredged material deposited in wetlands or waters
Tidal Restriction	Tidal flow limited by roadways, railroad embankments, undersized culverts, or similar structures
Transportation, Communications & Utilities	Roads, highways, railroads, powerlines, and similar structures
Unknown	Cause not determined
Urban	Development associated with towns and cities including golf courses and landfills
Vegetation Change	Succession; change in plant composition (specific species noted include _Iva frutescens_, _Phragmites australis_, _Typha angustifolia_)

Geospatial Database Construction and GIS Analysis

Geospatial database construction was performed by URI's Environmental Data Center (EDC). Each basemap was registered on the digitizing tablet with a RMS value ≤0.003. All features delineated for this project were digitized in ArcEdit and coded using ArcGIS 8.2 software. Data for each quad were digitized separately and joined to form one complete baywide coverage. Data for each USGS quadrangle were digitized, coded and proofed before moving on to the next quadrangle. Proofing took place in two phases: 1) on screen in ArcGIS 8.2 to check for coding errors as well as feature errors and 2) a proof plot of the linework information was made and sent along with the mylar basemap for NRAG to proof. Any feature omission or coding change was noted on the proof plot and returned to EDC for final editing.

The land use/cover data were digitized into an existing coverage containing the upland shoreline features from the coastal wetlands data layer and the 500-foot buffer line. Each quad was digitized and proofed separately to be *MAPJOINED* after all land use/cover data were completed. For those polygons coded as freshwater wetland, an item ENHANCED was added and attributed with a Cowardin et al. (1979) classification.

Upon construction of the final digital database, summary tables were generated by EDC using Arc/Info *FREQUENCY* command. These tables were used to prepare tables for this report (in the Results section and Appendices A and B). The database was used to prepare thematic maps showing wetland trends for the estuary and for each pilot area. The maps are presented in a separate folder and hyperlinked to the report.

Palmer River salt marsh (F. Golet photo)

Results

Baywide 1996 Status

Coastal Wetlands and Waters

In 1996, the Narragansett Bay Estuary (NBE) had 130,028 acres of tidal and subtidal saltwater-influenced habitats (Table 3). The Bay itself (estuarine and marine deepwater habitat) predominates this tidal ecosystem, accounting for 95% of this acreage. Intertidal habitats occupy only 5% of the estuary. Estuarine tidal marshes and swamps comprise 58% of this intertidal habitat, with the remainder made up mostly of nonvegetated tidal unconsolidated shores. The latter includes sandy beaches, sand and mud flats, and cobble-gravel shores. Nine acres of oyster reefs were inventoried.

Over 1,700 acres of vegetated coastal wetlands were altered by ditching and/or impoundment (Table 4). This acreage represented 48% of the NBE's coastal marshes (including estuarine scrub-shrub wetlands). Eighty-eight percent of this acreage was ditched. Only 36 acres of nonvegetated wetlands were altered. Fifteen acres of unconsolidated shore were created by spoil disposal, while nearly 5 acres of rocky shore were created by rip-rap (e.g., groins).

500-Foot Buffer Zone

The 500-foot buffer zone surrounding Narragansett Bay's coastal wetlands accounted for nearly 26,600 acres in 1996 (Table 5). Of this, 35% was represented by residential development (80% single family residences and 18% lawns). Forests and rangeland occupied 22% and 15% of the buffer, respectively. See Table 8 for more detailed findings.

Sachuset Point shoreline (F. Golet photo)

Table 3. 1996 status of coastal wetlands and waters in the Narragansett Bay Estuary. (<u>Note</u>: These data summarize totals for mapped polygons only; linear data are not included.) EM=emergent; US=Unconsolidated Shore.

Wetland or Waterbody Type	1990s Acreage
Estuarine Water	
Eelgrass Bed	93.1
Saline/Brackish	89,505.7
Oligohaline	143.2
--------------------	-----------
Subtotal	89,742.0
Estuarine Marsh	
Emergent Regularly Flooded	272.1
Phragmites Irregularly Flooded	217.0
EM/Phragmites Irregularly Flooded	14.7
EM/US Regularly Flooded	5.8
EM/US Irregularly Flooded	0.3
Emergent Irregularly Flooded	2,458.1
Phragmites/Shrub Irregularly Flooded	3.3
EM/Shrub Irregularly Flooded	6.9
--	------------
Subtotal	2,978.2
Estuarine Oligohaline Marsh	
Emergent Regularly Flooded	0.8
Phragmites Irregularly Flooded	142.0
EM/Phragmites Irregularly Flooded	115.5
Emergent Irregularly Flooded	172.9
-------------------------------------	-----------
Subtotal	431.2
Estuarine Scrub-Shrub Wetland	
Deciduous Irregularly Flooded	161.8
Shrub/EM Irregularly Flooded	0.7
--	-----------
Subtotal	162.5
Estuarine Reef	
Mollusc (Oyster)	9.3
Estuarine Streambed	
Sand and Mud Regularly Flooded	3.0

Table 3. (continued)

Estuarine Rocky Shore

Bedrock Regularly Flooded	29.1
Bedrock Irregularly Flooded	96.9
Rubble Regularly Flooded	76.6
Rubble Irregularly Flooded	16.1
------------------------------------	--------
Subtotal	218.7

Estuarine Unconsolidated Shore

Cobble-Gravel Regularly Flooded	68.2
Cobble-Gravel Irregularly Flooded	59.6
Sand Irregularly Exposed	254.4
Sand Regularly Flooded	443.5
Sand/Cobble-Gravel Regularly. Flooded	42.1
Sand/Emergent Regularly Flooded	5.9
Sand Irregularly Flooded	580.1
Mud Irregularly Exposed	200.4
Mud Irregularly. Exposed Oligohaline	0.9
Mud Regularly Flooded	105.5
Mud Regularly. Flooded Oligohaline	7.0
--	---------
Subtotal	1,767.6

Estuarine Salt Panne

Irregularly Exposed	39.5
Irregularly Exposed Oligohaline	0.8
Regularly Flooded	1.7
---	----------
Subtotal	42.0

Total Estuarine Habitat	***95,354.5***

Marine Water

Eelgrass Bed	2.6
Unconsolidated Bottom	34,130.3
--	-------------
Subtotal	34,132.9

Marine Rocky Shore

Regularly Flooded	142.5
Irregularly Flooded	202.2
--	------------
Subtotal	344.7

Table 3. (continued)

Marine Unconsolidated Shore

Cobble-Gravel Regularly Flooded	5.9
Cobble-Gravel Irregularly Flooded	9.6
Sand Irregularly Exposed	2.3
Sand Regularly Flooded	100.7
Sand Irregularly Flooded	77.2
Subtotal	195.7

Total Marine Habitats	***34,673.3***
Narragansett Bay Grand Total	**130,027.8**

Table 4. Extent of altered coastal wetlands for the Narragansett Bay Estuary in 1996.

Wetland Type	Type of Alteration	Acreage
Emergent		
Regularly Flooded	ditched	0.7
	impounded	6.2
	(subtotal)	(6.9)
Irregularly Flooded	ditched	1336.0
	ditched/impounded	115.2
	impounded	51.7
	(subtotal)	(1502.9)
Emergent Oligohaline		
Regularly Flooded	impounded	0.5
Irregularly Flooded	ditched	19.0
	ditched/impounded	5.6
	impounded	143.7
	(subtotal)	(168.3)
Reef	impounded	3.2
Rocky Shore	artificial	4.7
Scrub-Shrub	ditched	33.9
	ditched/impounded	1.6
	impounded	1.2
	(subtotal)	(36.7)
Unconsolidated Shore	ditched	3.7
	impounded	9.1
	spoil	15.0
	(subtotal)	(27.8)
All Types		1,751.0

Table 5. Land use/cover in the 500-foot buffer around coastal wetlands in the Narragansett Bay Estuary in 1996. (<u>Note</u>: % buffer totals 100.1% due to round-off procedures.)

Land Use/Cover	Acreage	% of Buffer
Residential	9,324.7	35.1
Commercial	2,235.5	8.4
Industrial	106.1	0.4
Transportation, Communications, Utilities	744.9	2.8
Other Urban or Built-up Land	845.7	3.2
Agriculture	1,507.5	5.7
Rangeland	3,965.2	14.9
Forest	5,734.9	21.6
Water and Freshwater Wetland	1,669.6	6.3
Barren Land	26,589.7	1.7
Total	26,589.7	100.1

Baywide Trends 1951/2 to 1996

Coastal Wetlands

From the 1950s to the 1990s, the NBE experienced a net loss of 548 acres of tidal habitat. The losses concentrated on intertidal habitats with 306 acres of net loss of estuarine marshes (excluding oligohaline marshes) and a net loss of 205 acres of intertidal nonvegetated wetlands (estuarine unconsolidated shores). During this period, 7.2% of the NBE's estuarine intertidal wetland acreage was lost. Nearly 10% of the estuarine marsh acreage (excluding oligohaline marshes) was lost. Almost 110 acres of coastal waters were lost. Details are provided in Table 6.

The nature and causes of coastal wetland changes are summarized in Table 7. Please note that a loss of a given wetland may be attributed to more than one cause, so the acreage totals from this table may be greater than the net acreage figures reported in Table 6. Causes of wetland changes are illustrated in Figures 4 through 7. Over 50% of the loss of estuarine marsh was due to filling that created upland (dryland) (Figure 4). Nearly 40% of the loss was attributed to conversion to open water (15%), palustrine wetland (12%), and tidal flats (11%). Nine percent of the loss was represented by acreage that changed to estuarine scrub-shrub wetland. While estuarine marshes experienced net losses, there were some gains in estuarine wetland acreage in places. Gains largely came from tidal flats and estuarine water which accounted for over 70% of the estuarine marsh acreage gained (Figure 5). Of the changes to estuarine scrub-shrub wetlands, nearly 60% was due to a gain from estuarine emergent wetland (Figure 6). Forty percent of the changes in these shrub swamps were losses to estuarine marshes (33%) and to upland (7%). Most of the change in estuarine nonvegetated flats and shores were losses (Figure 7). More acreage was converted to open water than came from open water (Table 7). This may be a sign of the impact of rising sea level associated with global warming. About 106 acres of nonvegetated coastal wetlands were converted to upland. (Note: See Appendix A for more detailed findings.)

The locations of these changes are shown on a series of maps. To access information for individual towns, click on the town name: Barrington, Bristol, Cranston, East Greenwich, East Providence, Jamestown, Little Compton, Middletown, Narragansett, Newport, North Kingstown, Pawtucket, Portsmouth, Providence, South Kingstown, Tiverton, Warren, and Warwick.

500-foot Buffer Zone Around Coastal Wetlands

Significant changes in the buffer occurred during the 40-year study interval. A 37% increase in residential land occurred largely at the expense of rangeland and agricultural land which decreased by 30% and 52%, respectively (Table 8). This increase was mostly (94%) attributed to a rise in single-family homes along the coastal wetlands, whereas 92% of the loss of agricultural land was from pasture and haylands.

Table 6. Trends in coastal wetlands and waters in the Narragansett Bay Estuary from the 1950s to the 1990s. (Note: These data summarize totals for mapped polygons only; linear data are not included.) EM=emergent; US=Unconsolidated Shore; Phrag=Phragmites australis.

Wetland or Waterbody Type	1950s Acreage	1990s Acreage	Net Change
Estuarine Water			
Saline/Brackish	89,680.9	89,598.8	-82.1
Oligohaline	170.6	143.2	-27.4
Subtotal	89,851.5	89,742.0	-109.5
Estuarine Marsh			
Emergent Regularly Flooded	309.7	272.1	-37.6
Phragmites Irregularly Flooded	129.5	217.0	+87.5
EM/Phrag Irregularly Flooded	18.7	14.7	-4.0
EM/US Regularly Flooded	7.9	5.8	-2.1
EM/US Irregularly Flooded	0.3	0.3	0
Emergent Irregularly Flooded	2,808.8	2,458.1	-350.7
Phrag/Shrub Irregularly Flooded	3.3	3.3	0
EM/Shrub Irregularly Flooded	5.9	6.9	+1.0
Subtotal	3,284.1	2,978.2	-305.9
Estuarine Oligohaline Marsh			
Emergent Regularly Flooded	3.3	0.8	-2.5
Phragmites Irregularly Flooded	68.7	142.0	+73.3
EM/Phrag Irregularly Flooded	41.6	115.5	+73.9
Emergent Irregularly Flooded	244.9	172.9	-72.0
Subtotal	358.5	431.2	+72.7
Estuarine Reef			
Mollusc (Oyster)	10.7	9.3	-1.4
Estuarine Rocky Shore			
Bedrock Regularly Flooded	29.2	29.1	-0.1
Bedrock Irregularly Flooded	97.1	96.9	-0.2
Rubble Regularly Flooded	76.7	76.6	-0.1
Rubble Irregularly Flooded	15.9	16.1	+0.2
Subtotal	218.9	218.7	-0.2

Table 6. (continued)

Estuarine Streambed			
Sand and Mud Regularly Flooded	2.0	3.0	+1.0

Estuarine Scrub-Shrub Wetland			
Deciduous Irregularly Flooded	143.6	161.8	+18.2
Shrub/EM Irregularly Flooded	0.7	0.7	0
--	-----------	-----------	---------
Subtotal	144.3	162.5	+18.2

Estuarine Unconsolidated Shore			
Cobble-Gravel Regularly Flooded	54.8	68.2	+13.4
Cobble-Gravel Irregularly Flooded	55.2	59.6	+4.4
Sand Irregularly Exposed	333.6	254.4	-79.2
Sand Regularly Flooded	445.7	443.5	-2.2
Sand/Cobble-Gravel Reg. Flooded	39.3	42.1	+2.8
Sand/Emergent Regularly Flooded	5.9	5.9	0
Sand/EM Irregularly Flooded	0.5	0	-0.5
Sand Irregularly Flooded	654.2	580.1	-74.1
Sand Reg. Flooded Oligohaline	82.1	0	-82.1
Sand Irreg. Flooded Oligohaline	3.5	0	-3.5
Mud Irregularly Exposed	226.2	200.4	-25.8
Mud Irreg. Exposed Oligohaline	0.9	0.9	0
Mud Regularly Flooded	68.0	105.5	+37.5
Mud Reg. Flooded Oligohaline	2.3	7.0	+4.7
--	--------------	--------------	---------
Subtotal	1,972.2	1,767.6	-204.6

Estuarine Salt Panne			
Irregularly Exposed	56.6	39.5	-17.1
Irregularly Exposed Oligohaline	0.8	0.8	0
Regularly Flooded	2.9	1.7	-1.2
-------------------------------------	---------	----------	--------
Subtotal	60.3	42.0	-18.3

Total Estuarine Habitat	**95,902.5**	**95,354.5**	**-548.0**

(Marine totals on following page)

Table 6. (continued)

Marine Water

Unconsolidated Bottom	34,133.7	34,132.9	-0.8
-------------------------------------	---------------	-------------	--------
Subtotal	34,133.7	34,132.9	-0.8

Marine Rocky Shore

Regularly Flooded	142.8	142.5	-0.3
Irregularly Flooded	201.9	202.2	+0.3
-------------------------------------	---------------	------------	--------
Subtotal	344.7	344.7	0

Marine Unconsolidated Shore

Cobble-Gravel Regularly Flooded	5.9	5.9	0
Cobble-Gravel Irregularly Flooded	9.6	9.6	0
Sand Irregularly Exposed	2.3	2.3	0
Sand Regularly Flooded	94.9	100.7	+5.8
Sand Irregularly Flooded	83.0	77.2	-5.8
-------------------------------------	---------------	------------	--------
Subtotal	195.7	195.7	0

Total Marine Habitats	***34,674.1***	***34,673.3***	***-0.8***

Narragansett Bay Grand Total	**130,564.9**	**130,027.6**	**-537.8**

Table 7. Nature and causes of coastal wetland changes in the Narragansett Bay Estuary from the 1950s to the 1990s. Note: The acreage of areas of change affected by multiple causes has been listed under each of the relevant causes, so acreage totals in this table exceed actual acreage of loss or gain for each coastal wetland type as reported in Table 6.

Wetland Type*	Acreage Affected	Gain From or Lost To	Major Causes (% of affected acreage)
E2EM	52.6	From open water	coastal processes (67), succession (15)
	87.1	From E2US	tidal restriction (48), coastal processes (37)
	33.4	From E2SS	Phragmites invasion (55), ditching (36)
	8.8	From P-wetland	tidal restriction (36), ditching (31), excavation/impoundment (23)
	16.4	From upland	coastal processes (48), unknown (28)
	50.9	To open water	coastal processes (49), tidal restriction (31)
	38.3	To E2US	coastal processes (85)
	0.5	To E2SB	coastal processes (100)
	78.8	To E2SS	Iva succession (61), succession following ditching (33)
	111.1	To P-wetland	ditching (41), tidal restriction (37), succession (11)
	189.8	To upland	rangeland (36), residential (19), commercial/services (14), transportation/utilities (13)
	280.6	Change in EM type	Phragmites (59), other succession (20), tidal restriction (9, excluding Phragmites)
E2SS	0.8	From E2US	coastal processes (100)
	78.8	From E2EM	Iva succession (61), succession/ ditching (33)
	33.1	To E2EM	Phragmites (56), succession/ ditching (36)
	6.0	To upland	commercial/services (33), forest (27), industrial/commercial (14), agriculture (9), residential (9)

Table 7. (continued)

Wetland Type*	Acreage Affected	Gain From or Lost To	Major Causes (% of affected acreage)
E2US	140.5	From open water	coastal processes (89)
	36.6	From E2EM	coastal processes (89)
	1.5	From E2RS	coastal processes (83)
	34.0	From upland	coastal processes (80)
	250.1	To open water	coastal processes (99)
	112.3	To E2EM	succession (40), tidal restriction (37), coastal processes (17)
	0.8	To E2SS	coastal processes (100)
	21.5	To P-wetland	tidal restriction (52), succession (44)
	105.3	To upland	golf course (33), rangeland (30), barren land (14), commercial/services (5)
	48.5	Change in Type	coastal processes (73)

----

*E2EM - estuarine emergent wetland; E2SS - estuarine scrub-shrub wetland; E2US - estuarine unconsolidated shore; E2SB - estuarine streambed; E2RS - estuarine rocky shore; P - palustrine.

Figure 4. Percent loss of estuarine emergent wetland in the Narragansett Bay Estuary.

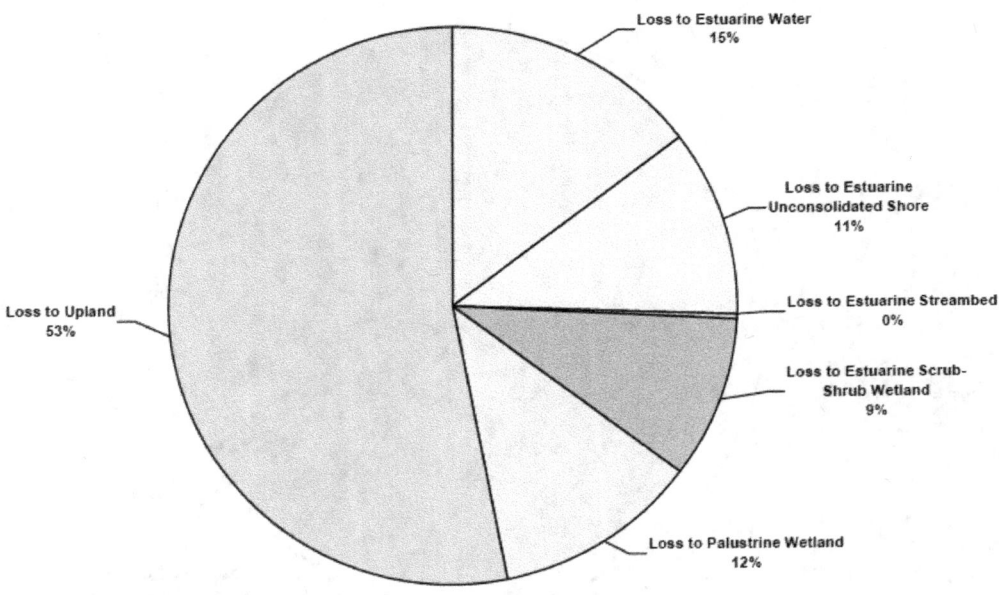

Loss to Estuarine Water
15%

Loss to Estuarine
Unconsolidated Shore
11%

Loss to Estuarine Streambed
0%

Loss to Estuarine Scrub-
Shrub Wetland
9%

Loss to Upland
53%

Loss to Palustrine Wetland
12%

Figure 5. Percent gain in estuarine emergent wetland in the Narragansett Bay Estuary.

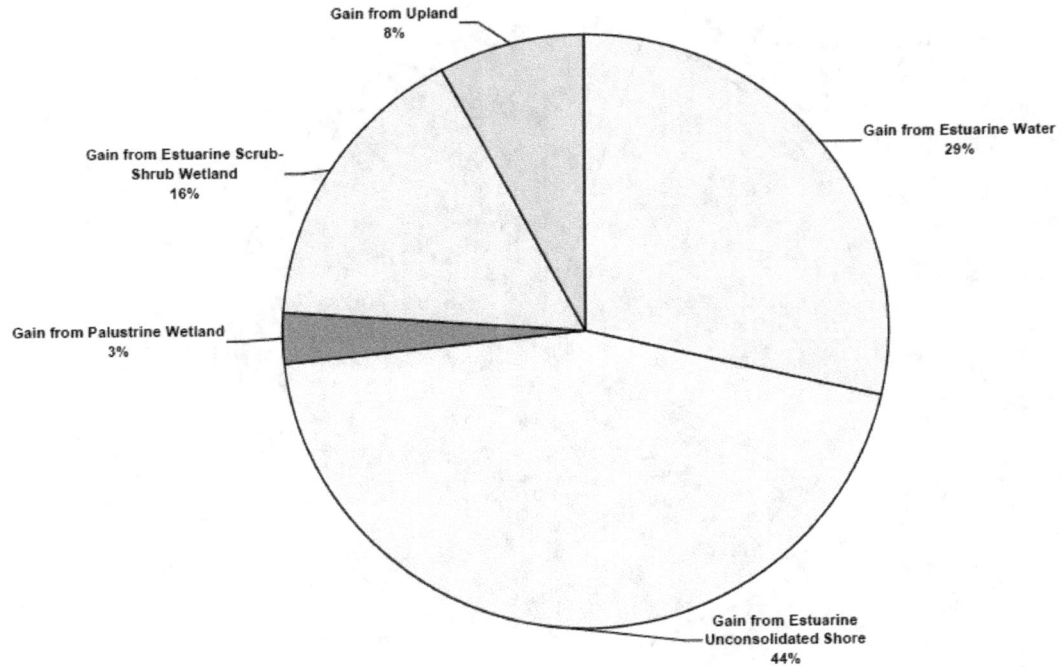

Gain from Upland
8%

Gain from Estuarine Scrub-
Shrub Wetland
16%

Gain from Palustrine Wetland
3%

Gain from Estuarine Water
29%

Gain from Estuarine
Unconsolidated Shore
44%

21

Figure 6. Percent change in estuarine scrub-shrub wetland in the Narragansett Bay Estuary.

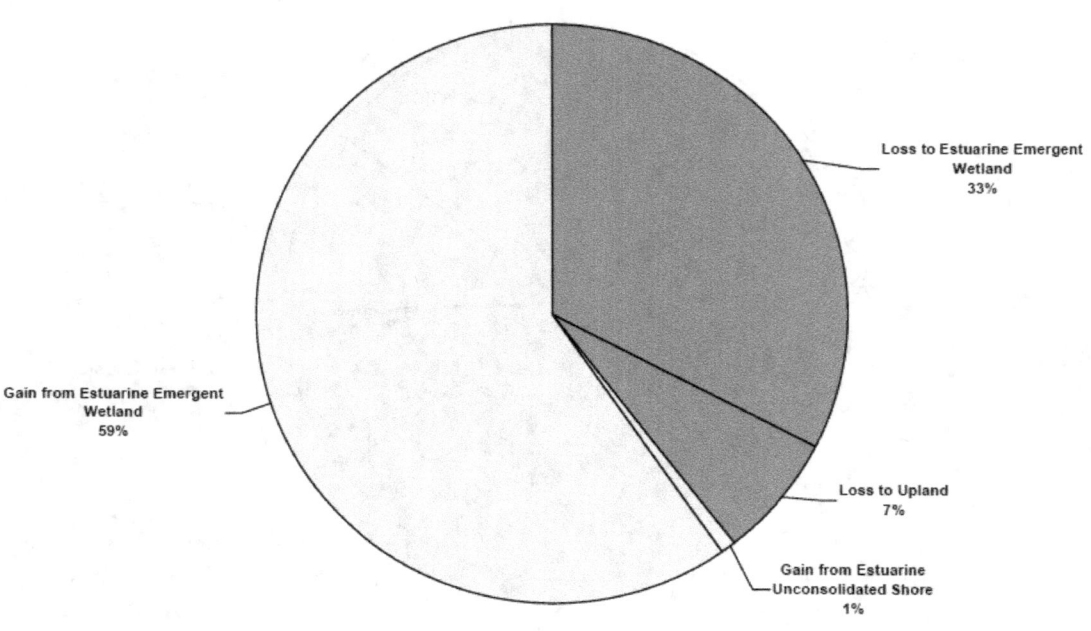

Loss to Estuarine Emergent Wetland
33%

Gain from Estuarine Emergent Wetland
59%

Loss to Upland
7%

Gain from Estuarine Unconsolidated Shore
1%

Figure 7. Percent change in estuarine unconsolidated shore in the Narragansett Bay Estuary.

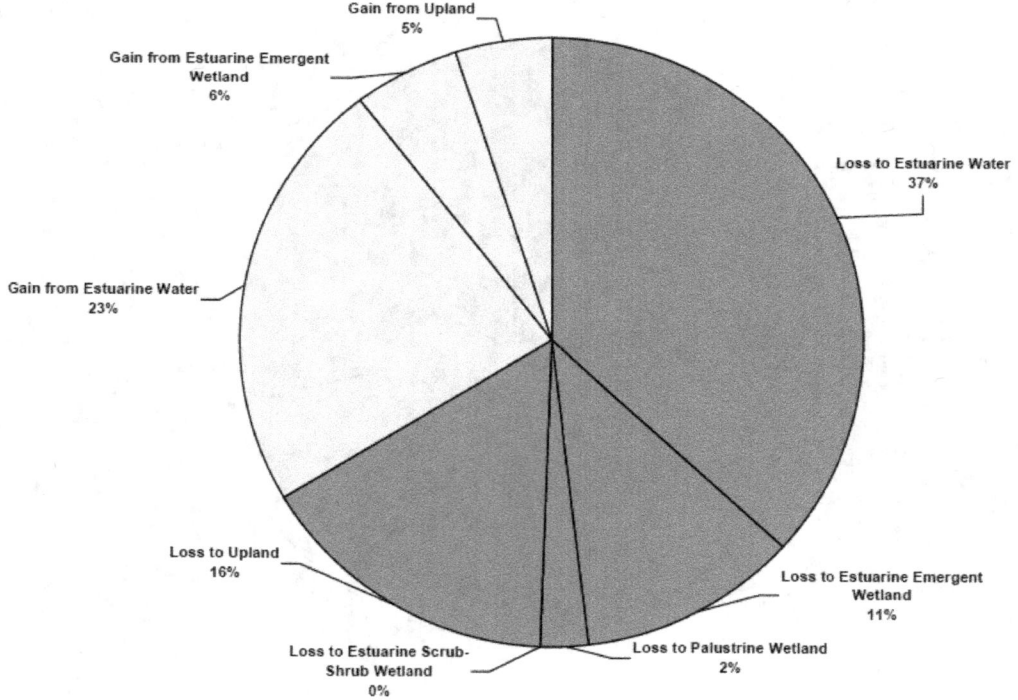

Gain from Upland
5%

Gain from Estuarine Emergent Wetland
6%

Gain from Estuarine Water
23%

Loss to Estuarine Water
37%

Loss to Upland
16%

Loss to Estuarine Emergent Wetland
11%

Loss to Estuarine Scrub-Shrub Wetland
0%

Loss to Palustrine Wetland
2%

Table 8. Land use/cover changes (acres and % of 1950s area) in the 500-foot buffer surrounding tidal wetlands in the Narragansett Bay Estuary from the 1950s to the 1990s. + = gain and - = loss

Land Use/cover Type	50s Acreage	90s Acreage	Acreage Change (% Change)
Residential			
Single-family	5,106.5	7,461.1	+2,354.6 (46)
Lawns	1,550.4	1,637.5	+87.1 (6)
Multi-family	36.4	177.8	+141.4 (389)
Mobile home	13.6	13.8	+0.2 (2)
Other	112.8	34.6	-78.2 (69)
Subtotal	*6,819.7*	*9,324.7*	*+2,505.0 (37)*
Commercial			
Comm.&Institutional Structures	871.3	1,104.5	+233.2 (27)
Wharves, Piers, Shipyards	567.2	561.7	+5.5 (1)
Paved Surfaces	131.7	261.2	+129.5 (98)
Marinas	134.1	206.2	+72.2 (54)
Unpaved Surfaces	91.0	49.2	-41.8 (46)
Recreational Structures	36.9	51.5	+4.6 (13)
Junkyard	0.1	0.1	0 (0)
Other	1.2	1.2	0 (0)
Subtotal	*1,843.5*	*2,235.5*	*+392.0 (21)*
Industrial	243.7	90.2	-153.5 (63)
Industrial & Commercial Complexes	23.8	15.9	-7.9 (33)
Transportation, Communications, & Utilities	409.5	744.9	+335.4 (82)
Other Urban or Built-up Land			
Golf Courses	273.6	420.7	+147.1 (54)
Landfills	18.3	38.8	+20.5 (112)
Cemetaries	52.5	56.3	+3.8 (7)
Other	148.6	329.9	+181.3 (122)
Subtotal	*493.0*	*845.7*	*+353.7 (72)*
Agriculture			
Pasture/hayfields	2,037.9	532.5	-1,505.4 (74)
Cropland	1,037.7	917.9	-119.8 (12)
Orchards, Nursuries, Vineyards	55.3	53.7	-1.6 (3)
Confined Feeding Lots	6.9	3.4	-3.5 (51)
Subtotal	*3,137.8*	*1,507.5*	*-1,630.3 (52)*

Table 8. (continued)

Land Use/cover Type	50s Acreage	90s Acreage	Acreage Change (% Change)
Rangeland			
Herbaceous	1,102.9	451.2	-651.7 (59)
Shrub and Brush	3,211.2	2,640.4	-570.9 (18)
Mixed	1,379.5	873.7	-505.9 (37)
Subtotal	*5,693.7*	*3,965.2*	*-1,728.5 (30)*
Forest			
Deciduous	2,212.1	2,309.8	+97.7 (44)
Evergreen	235.5	14.6	-220.9 (94)
Mixed	2,836.1	3,410.4	+574.3 (20)
Subtotal	*5,283.8*	*5,734.9*	*+451.1 (9)*
Water & Wetlands			
Vegetated Freshwater Wetland	1,390.7	1,486.2	+95.5 (7)
Nonvegetated Freshwater Wetland	8.0	11.5	+3.5 (44)
Fresh Water	171.9	172.0	+0.1 (1)
Subtotal	*1,570.6*	*1,669.6*	*+99.0 (6.3)*
Barren Land			
Beaches	19.1	0.9	-18.2 (95)
Other Sand Areas	188.9	129.5	-59.4 (31)
Mixed Barren Land	300.7	247.1	-53.6 (18)
Strip Mines	10.0	33.4	+23.4 (234)
Bare Exposed Rock	8.6	3.4	-5.2 (61)
Transitional Area	44.7	41.4	-3.3 (7)
Subtotal	*572.1*	*455.6*	*-116.5 (20)*

Trends for Pilot Study Areas

Wetland trends from the 1930s to the 1950s and the 1950s to the 1990s were examined for six study areas in the Narragansett Bay Estuary: 1) Allins Cove (including West Shore of Barrington), 2) Calf Pasture Point (North Kingstown), 3) Jacobs Point (Warren), 4) Palmer River (Warren), 5) Sachuest Point (Middletown), and 6) Wesquage Pond (Narragansett). All sites experienced net losses of coastal wetlands (Table 9). With a net loss of 104.0 acres, Calf Pasture Point lost the most coastal wetland acreage between the 1930s and the 1990s. Wesquage Pond was next ranked with a net loss of 52.6 acres, followed by Sachuest Point (net loss of 27.9 acres). The other areas experienced only minor net losses (Allins Cove - 7.4 acres; Jacobs Point - 4.4 acres; Palmer River - 0.7 acre). The nature and causes of changes in wetlands and deepwater habitats are presented for each study area in Tables 10 through 15. More detailed findings are given in Appendix B.

The location of these changes are documented on a series of maps showing trends from the 1930s to the 1950s and from the 1950s to the 1990s. To view the maps, <u>click here</u>.

Calf Pasture Point lost more acreage of coastal marsh prior to the 1950s, while it lost more unconsolidated shore (e.g., flats) since then (Table 11). In the earlier period, roughly 70 acres of marsh were lost, with 83% converted to upland; 17 acres of tidal flats were lost with about 14 acres filled (10 acres - commercial/services). Most of this new land was undeveloped in the 1950s (e.g., barren land and rangeland). The rest of the lost marsh was classified as irregularly flooded nonvegetated wetland (spoil deposits in the high marsh) which likely were converted to upland thereafter. From the 50s to the 90s, Calf Pasture Point lost 86 acres of tidal flat and 17 acres of coastal marsh. About 60% of the former losses resulted in an increase in estuarine open water possibly due to a combination of coastal processes (erosion) before the shoreline was stabilized. Filling at Calf Pasture Point created nonvegetated wetlands from open water during the earlier period (this operation was ongoing in the 1950s) and as more fill was deposited these areas were converted to upland. Most of the marsh loss in this area took place during the early stages of this filling operation. By the 1990s, much of the lost coastal marsh between the 1950s and 1990s had become palustrine <u>Phragmites</u> marsh.

Wesquage Pond lost most of its tidal flats prior to the 1950s, accounting for 87% of the losses between the 1930s and 1990s (Table 15). Nearly all of these losses were attributed to tidal restriction which converted intertidal flats mostly to estuarine open water (oligohaline). This action also affected tidal marshes contributing to about a one-acre gain and a five-acre change in tidal marsh type (i.e., some irregularly flooded wetland to regularly flooded marsh and creating oligohaline conditions). About five acres of tidal marshes were filled in Wesquage Pond between the 1950s and the 1990s, with most being undeveloped (rangeland) in the 1990s. About four acres of marsh became open water due to tidal restriction.

Sachuest Point lost most of its coastal wetlands from the 1950s to the 1990s (Table 14). Thirty-eight acres of emergent wetlands were filled during this time. Filling most likely took place prior to passage of the tidal wetland protection act. Spoil deposition was a major factor impacting wetlands from the 1930s into the 1950s. In the 1990s, much of this acreage remained undeveloped in shrub or herbaceous cover. Some filling also took place at Sachuest Point between the 1930s and 1950s with about 6 acres of tidal flat (estuarine unconsolidated shore) impacted.

High-tide bush marsh at Patience Island (F. Golet photo)

Table 9. Status and trends in coastal wetlands for specific study areas.

Study Area	Wetland Type*	1930s Acreage	1950s Acreage	Net Change in Acreage (% Change)	1990s Acreage	Net Change in Acreage (% Change)	Total Change 1930s-1990s (% Change)
Allins Cove	EEM	65.8	62.7	-3.2 (-5)	45.7	-17.0 (-27)	-20.1 (-31)
	EEMO	13.7	7.2	-6.5 (-47)	8.7	+1.5 (+21)	-5.0 (-37)
	ESS	1.1	0.4	-0.7 (-64)	5.9	+5.5 (+1375)	+4.8 (+436)
	EUS	22.3	20.2	-2.1 (-9)	35.2	+15.0 (+74)	+12.9 (+58)
Calf Pasture Point	EEM	128.1	66.8	-61.3 (-48)	50.1	-16.7 (-25)	-78.0 (-61)
	EEMO	18.5	18.8	+0.3 (+2)	14.9	-3.9 (-21)	-3.6 (-20)
	ESS	5.3	0	-5.3 (-100)	4.4	+4.4 (NA)	-0.9 (-17)
	EUS	42.5	100.0	+57.5 (+135)	20.8	-79.2 (-79)	-21.7 (-51)
	ERS	0.3	0.3	0	0.5	+0.2 (+67)	+0.2 (+67)
Jacobs Point	EEM	22.3	22.3	0	23.9	+1.6 (+7)	+1.6 (+7)
	EEMO	9.7	7.1	-2.6 (-27)	12.6	+5.5 (+78)	+2.9 (+30)
	ESS	12.7	12.7	0	1.8	-10.9 (-86)	-10.9 (-86)
	EUS	7.3	7.3	0	9.3	+2.0 (+27)	+2.0 (+27)
	ERS	0.7	0.7	0	0.7	0	0
Palmer River	EEM	214.9	212.7	-2.2 (-1)	219.3	+6.6 (+3)	+4.4 (+2)
	EEMO	1.2	0	-1.2 (-100)	0	0	-1.2 (100)
	ESS	15.2	15.2	0	9.0	-6.2 (-41)	-6.2 (-41)
	EUS	8.1	8.7	+0.6 (+8)	10.4	+1.7 (+20)	+2.3 (+28)

* EEM - estuarine emergent; EEMO - estuarine emergent oligohaline; ESS - estuarine scrub-shrub; EUS - estuarine unconsolidated shore; ERS - estuarine rocky shore; ESB - estuarine streambed; MUS - marine unconsolidated shore; MRS - marine rocky shore.

27

Table 9. (continued)

Study Area	Wetland Type	1930s Acreage	1950s Acreage	Net Change in Acreage (% Change)	1990s Acreage	Net Change in Acreage (% Change)	Total Change 1930s-1990s (% Change)
Sachuest Point	EEM	62.6	69.9	+7.3 (+12)	32.2	-37.7 (-54)	-30.4 (-49)
	EEMO	3.1	1.9	-1.2 (-39)	14.3	+12.4 (+653)	+11.2 (+361)
	ESS	5.3	0	-5.3 (-100)	0	0	-5.3 (-100)
	EUS	20.6	14.4	-6.2 (-30)	17.2	+2.8 (+19)	-3.4 (-17)
	ERS	2.0	2.0	0	2.0	0	0
	MUS	46.7	46.7	0	46.7	0	0
	MRS	34.4	34.4	0	34.4	0	0
Wesquage Pond	EEM	7.7	8.4	+0.7 (+9)	0	-8.4 (-100)	-7.7 (-100)
	EEMO	19.3	19.6	+0.3 (+2)	24.1	+4.5 (+23)	+4.8 (+25)
	ESS	0.4	0.3	-0.1 (-25)	0	-0.3 (-100)	-0.4 (-100)
	EUS	51.4	2.3	-49.1 (-96)	1.7	-0.6 (-26)	-49.7 (-97)
	EUS/EM	0.2	0.5	+0.3 (+150)	0	-0.5 (-100)	-0.2 (-100)
	ESB	0.2	0.2	0	0.6	+0.4 (+200)	+0.4 (+200)
	ERS	11.5	11.5	0	11.7	+0.2 (+2)	+0.2 (+2)
	MUS	11.8	11.8	0	11.8	0	0
	MRS	3.5	3.5	0	3.5	0	0

28

Table 10. Nature and causes of coastal wetland and deepwater habitat trends for Allins Cove.

Time Period	Wetland Type*	Change Type	Acreage	Causes
1930s-50s	NVW	loss	2.9	coastal processes, filling (residential development)
		gain	0.7	coastal processes
		type change	1.0	coastal processes
		no change	18.5	n/a
	VW	loss	11.0	coastal processes, filling (golf course)
		gain	0.6	coastal processes, unknown
		type change	0.7	Phragmites, unknown
		no change	69.0	n/a
	CW	loss	1.0	coastal processes, unknown
		gain	5.4	coastal processes
		no change	20.7	n/a
1950s-90s	NVW	loss	1.0	coastal processes
		gain	15.9	coastal processes, unknown
		type change	2.2	coastal processes
		no change	17.0	n/a
	VW	loss	14.0	tidal restriction, filling (golf course, residential development), coastal processes
		gain	4.1	coastal processes, Phragmites invasion
		type change	6.9	ditching/Iva succession, tidal restriction, Phragmites, unknown
		no change	46.2	n/a
	CW	loss	16.2	coastal processes, spoil deposition, Phragmites invasion
		no change	9.9	n/a

* NVW - nonvegetated wetland; VW - vegetated wetland; CW - coastal water (deepwater habitat); n/a - not applicable.

Table 11. Nature and causes of coastal wetland and deepwater habitat trends for Calf Pasture Point.

Time Period	Wetland Type*	Change Type	Acreage	Causes
1930s-50s	NVW	loss	17.1	filling (commercial/services, barren land), coastal processes
		gain	74.5	spoil deposition, coastal processes
		type change	0.6	spoil deposition
		no change	25.0	n/a
	VW	loss	70.3	filling (barren land, rangeland, commercial/services, spoil deposition), coastal processes, ditching/succession,
		gain	4.0	coastal processes, Phragmites, unknown
		type change	8.4	spoil deposition, unknown
		no change	73.2	n/a
	CW	loss	123.0	filling (spoil deposition, barren land, commercial/services), coastal processes, Phragmites invasion
		gain	6.1	coastal processes, tidal restriction
		no change	6.0	n/a
1950s-90s	NVW	loss	85.7	coastal processes, filling (rangeland)
		gain	6.2	coastal processes, spoil deposition
		type change	3.7	spoil deposition, coastal processes, jetty/groin removal
		no change	10.9	n/a
	VW	loss	17.2	Phragmites invasion, filling (forest, rangeland, landfill, golf course, spoil deposition), coastal processes, tidal restriction
		gain	8.5	coastal processes, succession/ditching
		type change	28.3	succession/ditching, Phragmites, Iva, spoil deposition, unknown
		no change	40.1	n/a
	CW	loss	5.1	coastal processes, excavation
		gain	54.8	coastal processes
		no change	5.3	n/a

*NVW - nonvegetated wetland; VW - vegetated wetland; CW - coastal water (deepwater habitat); n/a - not applicable.

Table 12. Nature and causes of coastal wetland and deepwater habitat trends for Jacobs Point.

Time Period	Wetland Type*	Change Type	Acreage	Causes
1930s-50s	NVW	no change	8.0	n/a
	VW	loss	2.6	agriculture, tidal restriction/agriculture
		no change	29.4	n/a
	CW	no change	0.6	n/a
1950s-90s	NVW	loss	1.4	coastal processes
		gain	0.6	coastal processes
		no change	8.0	n/a
	VW	loss	3.8	filling (rangeland, residential development), coastal processes,
		type change	14.5	succession/ditching, Phragmites, Iva
		no change	23.8	n/a
	CW	loss	0.6	coastal processes

*NVW - nonvegetated wetland; VW - vegetated wetland; CW - coastal water (deepwater habitat); n/a - not applicable.

31

Table 13. Nature and causes of coastal wetland and deepwater habitat trends for Palmer River.

Time Period	Wetland Type*	Change Type	Acreage	Causes
1930s-50s	NVW	gain	0.6	unknown
		no change	8.1	n/a
	VW	loss	3.4	tidal restriction, filling (commercial/services, barren land, residential), coastal processes
		no change	227.9	n/a
	CW	loss	39.7	impoundment
		gain	0.5	coastal processes
		no change	10.0	n/a
1950s-90s	NVW	gain	2.2	coastal processes, unknown
		loss	0.6	unknown
		no change	8.1	n/a
	VW	gain	3.8	coastal processes, spoil deposition, succession/ditching, unknown
		loss	3.3	filling (residential development, commercial/services, rangeland)
		type change	21.0	Phragmites, succession/ditching, Iva, unknown
	CW	no change	203.6	n/a
		loss	8.0	filling (rangeland, commercial/services, residential development), coastal processes, succession/ditching, unknown

* NVW - nonvegetated wetland; VW - vegetated wetland; CW - coastal water (deepwater habitat); n/a - not applicable.

32

Table 14. Nature and causes of coastal wetland and deepwater habitat trends for Sachuest Point.

Time Period	Wetland Type*	Change Type	Acreage	Causes
1930s-50s	NVW	loss	6.2	filling (spoil deposition, commercial/services), coastal processes, Phragmites invasion
		no change	97.5	n/a
	VW	loss	4.8	filling (residential, transportation/comm./utilities, commercial/services)
		gain	5.7	spoil deposition, Phragmites invasion, coastal processes
		type change	29.0	spoil deposition
		no change	37.2	n/a
	CW	no change	2.2	n/a
1950s-90s	NVW	gain	2.8	coastal processes
		type change	1.9	coastal processes
		no change	95.5	n/a
	VW	loss	26.3	filling (spoil deposition, rangeland, commercial/services, barren land)
		gain	1.0	revegetation (sediment accretion after excavation)
		type change	20.6	tidal restriction, Phragmites invasion, succession/ditching
		no change	24.9	n/a
	CW	loss	1.6	revegetation (excavation), coastal processes
		no change	0.6	n/a

*NVW - nonvegetated wetland; VW - vegetated wetland; CW - coastal water (deepwater habitat); n/a - not applicable.

33

Table 15. Nature and causes of coastal wetland and deepwater habitat trends for Wesquage Pond.

Time Period	Wetland Type*	Change Type	Acreage	Causes
1930s-50s	NVW	loss	49.1	tidal restriction, coastal processes
		gain	0.3	coastal processes
		no change	29.5	n/a
	VW	loss	0.4	filled (commercial)
		gain	1.5	tidal restriction, coastal processes
		type change	5.0	tidal restriction, Phragmites
		no change	21.9	n/a
	CW	loss	0.5	coastal processes, tidal restriction
		gain	47.6	tidal restriction
		no change	20.5	n/a
1950s-90s	NVW	loss	1.1	filling (residential development)
		gain	0.7	coastal processes, jetty/groin construction
		no change	28.7	n/a
	VW	loss	9.2	tidal restriction, filling (commercial/services, rangeland, residential)
		gain	5.0	tidal restriction, Phragmites, unknown
		type change	4.0	tidal restriction, Phragmites, unknown
		no change	15.0	n/a
	CW	loss	5.7	tidal restriction, Phragmites, filling (residential), jetty/groin construction, unknown
		gain	4.4	tidal restriction
		type change	0.3	impounded/tidal restriction
		no change	62.1	n/a

* NVW - nonvegetated wetland; VW - vegetated wetland; CW - coastal water (deepwater habitat); na - not applicable.

34

Conclusions

The Narragansett Bay Estuary (NBE) contains about 130,000 acres of tidal and subtidal habitats. Open water is the predominant feature of the Bay occupying about 95% of the tidal ecosystem. Intertidal habitats (marshes, beaches, flats, and other shores) represent only 5% of the ecosystem. Of this, vegetated wetlands (mostly salt marshes) comprise 58% of the acreage, with the rest made up mostly of tidal flats. Nine acres of oyster reefs were inventoried. Over 1,700 acres (or 48%) of the coastal marshes have been ditched and/or impounded. Slightly more than one-third of the 500-foot buffer around the coastal wetlands is occupied by residential development. Forests and rangeland (i.e., fields and shrub thickets) represent 22% and 15% of the buffer, respectively.

Between the 1950s and 1990s, the NBE lost a net total of about 110 acres of estuarine open water, nearly 306 acres of salt and brackish marshes, and 205 acres of intertidal shores. A net gain of 73 acres of slightly brackish marshes took place, mostly at the expense of more saline wetlands. About 190 acres of salt/brackish marshes were filled. Common reed (<u>Phragmites</u> <u>australis</u>), a widespread invasive grass, increased its distribution during the study period by roughly 240 acres. Major causes of coastal marsh loss and degradation were filling and tidal restriction. Gains and losses of coastal marsh attributed to coastal processes (erosion/accretion) were nearly even, where these processes caused about 1.5 times more loss of unconsolidated shores than gains between the 1950s and 1990s.

For six areas in the NBE, wetlands trends were examined back to the 1930s (Allins Cove, Calf Pasture Point, Jacobs Point, Palmer River, Sachuest Point, and Wesquage Pond). All sites experienced net losses of coastal wetlands, but only Calf Pasture Point (104 acres), Wesquage Pond (53 acres), and Sachuest Point (28 acres) lost more than 10 acres. The other areas lost less than eight acres each.

Acknowledgments

Funding for this project was provided by the Narragansett Bay Estuary Program (NBEP). Helen Cottrell served as project officer for NBEP. She reviewed the draft manuscript and products and provided photographs for use in this report. Ralph Tiner was project officer for the U.S Fish and Wildlife Service (FWS). He was responsible for study design, project oversight, data analysis and synthesis, and report preparation.

Wetland trends data were collected by the Natural Resources Assessment Group (NRAG) in the Department of Plant and Soil Sciences, University of Massachusetts-Amherst, under the direction of Dr. Peter Veneman, principal investigator. Most of the photointerpretation and cartographic work was performed by Irene Huber and Todd Nuerminger. Mary Johnson (NRAG) assisted in photointerpretation of land use/cover trends in the 500-foot buffer around coastal wetlands. Craig Polzen also did some work on this photo-analysis and provided GIS support to NRAG.

Digital database construction and GIS analyses were accomplished by Aimée Mandeville of the University of Rhode Island's Environmental Data Center. She digitized map overlay products to create the geospatial database, performed analytical inquiries, and produced color-coded maps and statistical summaries presented in this report including the Appendices. Figure 1 was prepared by Paul Jordan, Rhode Island Department of Environmental Management, Geographic Information System Program, while Aimée created Figures 2 and 3. Herbert Bergquist (FWS) assisted in preparing the cover of this report, while Lorraine Fox (FWS) scanned the photos for conversion to digital images. Dr. Frank Golet, University of Rhode Island, gratiously provided color photographs of coastal wetlands for use in this report.

.

References

Anderson, J.R., E.E. Hardy, J.T. Roach, and R.E. Witmer. 1976. A Land Use and Land Cover Classification System for Use with Remote Sensor Data. U.S. Geological Survey Professional Paper 96A, U.S. Government Printing Office, Washington, DC.

Cowardin, L.W., V. Carter, F.C. Golet, and E.T. LaRoe. 1979. Classification of Wetlands and Deepwater Habitats of the United States. U.S. Fish and Wildlife Service, Washington, DC.

Huber, I. and T. Nuerminger. 2003. Rhode Island Narragansett Bay Project Area: Trends Analysis Methodology. Department of Plant and Soil Sciences, Natural Resources Assessment Group, University of Massachusetts, Amherst, MA.

Appendices

Click here for Appendices

Appendix A. Baywide Summary Tables for the Narragansett Bay Estuary.

Table 1-A. Changes in estuarine emergent wetlands in the Narragansett Bay Estuary: 1950s to 1990s. (Note: Acreage totals reflect acreage affected by each cause so there is double counting of some lost acreage; totals are greater than the actual total loss for these wetlands.)

Table 2-A. Changes in estuarine scrub-shrub wetlands in the Narragansett Bay Estuary: 1950s to 1990s. (Note: Acreage totals reflect acreage affected by each cause so there is double counting of some lost acreage; totals are greater than the actual total loss for these wetlands.)

Table 3-A. Changes in estuarine unconsolidated shores (beaches and tidal flats) in the Narragansett Bay Estuary: 1950s to 1990s. (Note: Acreage totals reflect acreage affected by each cause so there is double counting of some lost acreage; totals are greater than the actual total loss for these wetlands.)

Table 4-A. Changes in vegetated coastal wetlands in the Narragansett Bay Estuary: 1950s to 1990s. (Changes arranged by unique vegetated wetland types; no double counting.)

Table 5-A. Changes in nonvegetated coastal wetlands in the Narragansett Bay Estuary: 1950s to 1990s. (Changes arranged by unique types; no double counting.)

Note: "Coastal processes" includes erosion and accretion related to wave and current action and to sea level changes.

Table 1-A. Changes in estuarine emergent wetlands in the Narragansett Bay Estuary: 1950s to 1990s. (Note: Acreage totals reflect acreage affected by each cause so there is double counting of some lost acreage; totals are greater than the actual total loss for these wetlands.)

Type of Change	Cause of Change	Number of sites	Acres
Loss to Estuarine Water (E1UB*)			
	Boat Traffic	7	5.46
	Coastal processes	29	24.69
	Tidal restriction	10	15.93
	Unknown	4	4.80
Total		**50**	**50.88**
Loss to Estuarine Nonvegetated Wetland (E2US*)			
	Coastal processes	31	32.68
	Unknown	7	5.59
Total		**38**	**38.27**
Loss to Estuarine Vegetated Streambed (E2SB*)			
	Coastal processes	1	0.54
Total		**1**	**0.54**
Loss to Estuarine Vegetated Wetland (E2SS*)			
	Iva frutescens succession	31	47.82
	Succession following ditching	11	25.89
	Tidal restriction	1	0.80
	Unknown	1	4.29
Total		**44**	**78.80**
Loss to Palustrine Wetland (P_*)			
	Coastal processes	1	1.09
	Iva frutescens succession	1	1.88
	Phragmites australis invasion	2	6.31
	Succession	6	10.24
	Succession following ditching	15	46.04
	Tidal restriction	18	39.82
	Tidal restriction w/ P. australis invasion	1	1.23
	Unknown	6	4.47
Total		**50**	**111.08**
Loss to Upland			
	Agriculture (cropland)	1	3.46
	Agriculture (orchards, nurseries, vineyards, ornamental horticulture)	1	0.47
	Agriculture (pasture and hayfields)	1	0.73
	Barren Land (mixed barren land)	2	4.02
	Barren Land (sand areas other than beaches)	3	7.35

Barren Land (strip mines, quarries and gravel pits)	1	0.41
Commercial and Services (commercial and institutional structures)	4	3.34
Commercial and Services (marinas)	4	12.55
Commercial and Services (paved surfaces)	4	3.38
Commercial and Services (recreational structures)	1	3.05
Commercial and Services (unpaved surfaces)	3	2.47
Commercial and Services (wharves, piers & shipyards)	1	1.16
Forest (deciduous)	3	3.31
Forest (mixed)	4	5.11
Industrial & Commercial Complexes	1	2.15
Rangeland (herbaceous cover)	4	14.96
Rangeland (mixed)	3	9.85
Rangeland (shrub and brush cover)	17	42.71
Residential (lawns)	7	13.21
Residential (single family)	7	22.64
Transportation, Communications and Utilities	3	25.20
Unknown	2	0.83
Urban (golf courses)	5	5.86
Urban (landfills)	1	1.61

Total   **83**   **189.82**
Grand Total Loss (all losses combined)   469.39
Gain from Estuarine Water (E1UB*)

Coastal processes	47	34.99
Excavation re-vegetated	2	1.27
P. australis and Typha angustifolia invasion	2	1.76
Phragmites australis invasion	2	0.82
Succession	1	0.41
Succession following ditching	5	2.19
Tidal restriction	3	1.47
Tidal restriction w/ P. australis invasion	4	6.48
Unknown	3	3.23

Total   **69**   **52.63**

Gain from Estuarine Nonvegetated Wetland (E2US*)

	Coastal processes	24	32.49
	P. australis & Typha angustifolia invasion	1	0.83
	Phragmites australis invasion	2	1.61
	Succession	2	2.40
	Succession following ditching	3	5.30
	Tidal restriction	1	42.03
	Unknown	4	2.46
Total		**37**	**87.12**

Gain from Estuarine Vegetated Wetland (E2SS*)

	Coastal processes	1	0.26
	P. australis & Typha angustifolia invasion	1	3.31
	Phragmites australis invasion	6	15.07
	Succession following ditching	5	11.94
	Tidal restriction	1	0.29
	Unknown	3	2.53
Total		**17**	**33.40**

Gain from Palustrine Wetland (P_*)

	Excavation	1	1.06
	Impoundment	1	0.96
	Phragmites australis invasion	1	0.96
	Succession following ditching	2	2.69
	Tidal restriction w/ P. australis invasion	2	3.12
Total		**7**	**8.80**

Gain from Upland

	Coastal processes	7	7.83
	Phragmites australis invasion	3	1.50
	Succession following ditching	2	1.17
	Tidal restriction	1	1.00
	Tidal restriction w/ P. australis invasion	1	0.34
	Unknown	3	4.56
Total		**17**	**16.40**

Changes in Vegetated Type

	Coastal processes	1	0.14
	Iva frutescens succession	1	1.04
	P. australis & Typha angustifolia invasion	17	35.7
	Phragmites australis invasion	57	82.18
	Succession following ditching	28	54.61
	Tidal restriction	8	25.39
	Tidal restriction w/ P. australis invasion	27	47.51
	Unknown	28	33.99
Total		**167**	**280.56**

Table 2-A. Changes in estuarine scrub-shrub wetlands in the Narragansett Bay Estuary: 1950s to 1990s. (<u>Note</u>: Acreage totals reflect acreage affected by each cause so there is double counting of some lost acreage; totals are greater than the actual total loss for these wetlands.)

Type of Change	Cause of Change	Number of sites	Acres
Loss to Estuarine Emergent Wetland (E2EM*)			
	Succession following ditching	5	11.94
	Phragmites australis invasion	6	15.07
	P. australis and *Typha angustifolia* invasion	1	3.31
	Unknown	3	2.53
	Tidal restriction	1	0.29
Total		**16**	**33.14**
Loss to Upland			
	Agriculture (cropland)	1	0.55
	Commercial and Services (commercial and institutional structures)	1	0.80
	Commercial and Services (paved surfaces)	1	0.87
	Commercial and Services (recreational structures)	1	0.33
	Forest (mixed)	1	1.63
	Industrial & Commercial Complexes	1	0.86
	Rangeland (shrub and brush cover)	1	0.38
	Residential (single family)	1	0.54
Total		**8**	**5.97**
Gain from Estuarine Nonvegetated Wetland (E2US*)			
	Coastal processes	1	0.77
Total		**1**	**0.77**
Gain from Estuarine Vegetated Wetland (E2EM*)			
	Succession following ditching	11	25.89
	Iva frutescens succession	31	47.82
	Tidal restriction	1	0.80
	Unknown	1	4.29
Total		**44**	**78.80**

Table 3-A. Changes in estuarine unconsolidated shores (beaches and tidal flats) in the Narragansett Bay Estuary: 1950s to 1990s. (Note: Acreage totals reflect acreage affected by each cause so there is double counting of some lost acreage; totals are greater than the actual total loss for these wetlands.)

Type of Change	Cause of Change	Number of sites	Acres
Loss to Estuarine Water (E1UB*)			
	Coastal processes	50	248.63
	Unknown	2	1.46
Total		**52**	**250.09**
Loss to Estuarine Emergent Vegetated Wetland (E2EM*)			
	Coastal processes	18	19.08
	Succession following ditching	1	3.28
	Phragmites australis invasion	2	1.61
	Succession	3	44.42
	Tidal restriction	1	42.03
	Unknown	3	1.86
Total		**28**	**112.27**
Loss to Estuarine Scrub-Shrub Vegetated Wetland (E2SS*)			
	Coastal processes	1	0.77
Total		**1**	**0.77**
Loss to Palustrine Wetland (P_*)			
	Succession	3	9.44
	Tidal restriction	2	3.10
	Tidal restriction w/ P. australis invasion	2	8.01
	Unknown	1	0.97
Total		**8**	**21.52**
Loss to Upland			
	Agriculture (other)	1	7.92
	Barren Land (mixed barren land)	2	2.71
	Barren Land (sand areas other than beaches)	3	11.88
	Commercial and Services (marinas)	4	4.04
	Commercial and Services (paved surfaces)	2	0.75
	Forest (mixed)	2	1.00
	Industrial	1	1.19
	Rangeland (mixed)	5	24.17

	Rangeland (shrub and brush cover)	4	7.78
	Residential (single family)	7	2.71
	Transportation, Communications and Utilities	3	6.73
	Urban (golf courses)	5	34.40
Total		**39**	**105.28**
Gain from Estuarine Water (E1UB*)			
	Coastal processes	90	125.60
	Tidal restriction	8	5.64
	Unknown	9	9.27
Total		**107**	**140.51**
Gain from Estuarine Emergent Vegetated Wetland (E2EM*)			
	Coastal processes	31	32.68
	Unknown	5	3.88
Total		**36**	**36.56**
Gain from Estuarine Reef or Rocky Shore (E2R*)			
	Coastal processes	3	1.24
	Jetty/groin removal	1	0.26
Total		**4**	**1.49**
Gain from Upland			
	Coastal processes	18	27.15
	Jetty/groin removal	1	0.52
	Unknown	5	6.29
Total		**24**	**33.96**
Changes in Nonvegetated Type			
	Coastal processes	38	35.37
	Unknown	3	13.16
Total		**41**	**48.53**

Table 4-A. Changes in vegetated coastal wetlands in the Narragansett Bay Estuary: 1950s to 1990s.

Type of Change	1950s Type	1990s Type	Cause of Change	Number of Sites	Acres
Loss of Vegetated Coastal Wetland					
	E2EM1/US2N	E1UBL	Coastal processes	1	2.07
	Subtotal loss			**1**	**2.07**
	E2EM1N	DUNE	Coastal processes	1	1.35
	E2EM1N	E1UBL	Boat Traffic	4	2.91
	E2EM1N	E1UBL	Coastal processes	8	8.43
	E2EM1N	E1UBL	Unknown	1	3.62
	E2EM1N	E2US2P	Coastal processes	4	3.02
	E2EM1N	E2US2P	Unknown	1	0.26
	E2EM1N	E2US3M	Coastal processes	2	2.86
	E2EM1N	E2US3N	Unknown	1	0.37
	E2EM1N	UPLAND	Residential (single family)	1	0.45
	E2EM1N	UPLAND	Residential (lawns)	1	0.91
	E2EM1N	UPLAND	Commercial and Services (marinas)	4	2.12
	E2EM1N	UPLAND	Forest (mixed)	1	0.58
	Subtotal loss			**29**	**26.87**
	E2EM1Nh	E1UBL6h	Tidal restriction	5	4.42
	E2EM1Nh	E1UBLh	Tidal restriction	2	2.84
	Subtotal loss			**7**	**7.26**
	E2EM1P	DUNE	Coastal processes	6	3.86
	E2EM1P	E1UBL	Boat traffic	3	2.56
	E2EM1P	E1UBL	Coastal processes	14	11.45
	E2EM1P	E1UBL	Unknown	3	1.18

E2EM1P	E2SB3N	Coastal processes	1	0.54
E2EM1P	E2US2/1N	Coastal processes	1	1.31
E2EM1P	E2US2N	Coastal processes	4	6.04
E2EM1P	E2US2Ns	Coastal processes	1	2.47
E2EM1P	E2US2P	Coastal processes	4	2.97
E2EM1P	E2US2P	Unknown	3	3.24
E2EM1P	E2US3M	Coastal processes	10	10.47
E2EM1P	PAB4Vh	Tidal restriction	1	0.32
E2EM1P	PEM1E	Tidal restriction	1	0.24
E2EM1P	PEM1Rh	Tidal restriction	1	0.63
E2EM1P	PFO1C	Succession	1	0.53
E2EM1P	PSS1/EM1R	Succession	1	3.83
E2EM1P	PSS1R	Coastal processes	1	1.09
E2EM1P	PSS1R	Tidal restriction	1	1.04
E2EM1P	PSS1R	Succession	2	3.81
E2EM1P	PSS1Rd	Succession following ditching	1	3.41
E2EM1P	UPLAND	Agriculture (cropland)	2	3.46
E2EM1P	UPLAND	Agriculture (pasture and hayfields)	2	0.73
E2EM1P	UPLAND	Barren Land (mixed barren land)	2	2.80
E2EM1P	UPLAND	Barren Land (sand areas other than beaches)	5	5.65
E2EM1P	UPLAND	Barren Land (strip mines, quarries and gravel pits)	1	0.41
E2EM1P	UPLAND	Commercial and Services (commercial and institutional structures)	2	1.46
E2EM1P	UPLAND	Commercial and Services (marinas)	10	7.53
E2EM1P	UPLAND	Commercial and Services (paved surfaces)	2	1.77
E2EM1P	UPLAND	Commercial and Services (recreational structures)	2	3.05
E2EM1P	UPLAND	Commercial and Services (unpaved surfaces)	3	1.32
E2EM1P	UPLAND	Forest (deciduous)	1	1.01
E2EM1P	UPLAND	Forest (mixed)	2	0.73
E2EM1P	UPLAND	Rangeland (herbaceous cover)	4	6.88
E2EM1P	UPLAND	Rangeland (mixed)	8	8.53
E2EM1P	UPLAND	Rangeland (shrub and brush cover)	19	16.32
E2EM1P	UPLAND	Residential (lawns, includes non-residential lawns)	10	9.76
E2EM1P	UPLAND	Residential (single family)	18	15.36
E2EM1P	UPLAND	Transportation, Communications and Utilities	11	22.40
E2EM1P	UPLAND	Unknown	1	0.52
E2EM1P	UPLAND	Urban (golf courses)	4	4.64
E2EM1P	UPLAND	Urban (landfills)	1	1.61

Code	Class	Description	Count	Area
Subtotal loss			**170**	**176.89**
E2EM1P6	E1UBL	Coastal processes	1	0.34
E2EM1P6	E2US4M	Unknown	1	1.41
E2EM1P6	PEM5R	*Phragmites australis invasion*	1	5.42
E2EM1P6	PSS1R	Unknown	1	0.48
E2EM1P6	PUBH	Tidal restriction	1	0.31
E2EM1P6	UPLAND	Forest (deciduous)	1	1.04
E2EM1P6	UPLAND	Forest (mixed)	2	3.80
E2EM1P6	UPLAND	Rangeland (shrub and brush cover)	2	2.41
E2EM1P6	UPLAND	Unknown	1	0.30
E2EM1P6	UPLAND	Urban (golf courses)	2	0.88
Subtotal loss			**13**	**16.39**
E2EM1P6d	PFO1R	Succession following ditching	1	0.29
E2EM1P6d	PSS1R	Succession following ditching	2	1.32
E2EM1P6d	PUBVh	Tidal restriction	1	0.39
E2EM1P6d	UPLAND	Rangeland (shrub and brush cover)	1	0.71
E2EM1P6d	UPLAND	Residential (lawns,includes non-residential lawns)	1	0.47
Subtotal loss			**6**	**3.17**
E2EM1P6dh	PEM1F	Succession following ditching & Tidal restriction	1	0.31
E2EM1P6dh	PEM1Rh	Succession following ditching & Tidal restriction	1	6.99
E2EM1P6dh	PFO1C	Succession following ditching & Tidal restriction	1	1.97
E2EM1P6dh	PSS1Eh	Succession following ditching & Tidal restriction	1	6.93
E2EM1P6dh	UPLAND	Commercial and Services (commercial and institutional structures)	1	0.54
E2EM1P6dh	UPLAND	Commercial and Services (paved surfaces)	1	0.26
Subtotal loss			**6**	**17.00**
E2EM1P6h	PFO1C	Tidal restriction	1	1.30
E2EM1P6h	PFO1R	Tidal restriction	1	1.19
E2EM1P6h	PSS1R	Tidal restriction	1	1.07
E2EM1P6h	UPLAND	Commercial and Services (commercial and institutional structures)	1	1.35
E2EM1P6h	UPLAND	Commercial and Services (paved surfaces)	2	1.35
E2EM1P6h	UPLAND	Residential (single family)	1	1.80
Subtotal loss			**7**	**8.04**

Code	Type	Description	Count	Value
E2EM1Pd	E1UBL	Coastal processes	5	2.37
E2EM1Pd	E1UBLh	Tidal restriction	1	3.16
E2EM1Pd	E2US2P	Coastal processes	4	2.23
E2EM1Pd	PEM1Rh	Succession following ditching & Tidal restriction	1	4.25
E2EM1Pd	PEM5/SS1R	Tidal restriction w/ P. australis invasion & Succession following ditching	1	1.23
E2EM1Pd	PFO1R	Succession following ditching	1	1.96
E2EM1Pd	PFO1R	Succession following ditching & Iva frutescens succession	1	1.88
E2EM1Pd	PSS1/EM5R	Succession following ditching & Phragmites australis invasion	1	0.89
E2EM1Pd	PSS1R	Succession following ditching	2	1.49
E2EM1Pd	PSS1R	Unknown	1	0.47
E2EM1Pd	PSS1Rd	Succession following ditching	1	2.74
E2EM1Pd	PUBVh	Succession following ditching & Tidal restriction	2	10.33
E2EM1Pd	UPLAND	Agriculture (orchards, nurseries, vineyards, ornamental horticulture)	1	0.47
E2EM1Pd	UPLAND	Barren Land (sand areas other than Beaches)	2	1.03
E2EM1Pd	UPLAND	Commercial and Services (marinas)	1	1.46
E2EM1Pd	UPLAND	Commercial and Services (unpaved surfaces)	1	1.15
E2EM1Pd	UPLAND	Industrial & Commercial Complexes	1	2.15
E2EM1Pd	UPLAND	Rangeland (herbaceous cover)	1	0.31
E2EM1Pd	UPLAND	Rangeland (shrub and brush cover)	5	8.30
E2EM1Pd	UPLAND	Residential (lawns, includes non-residential lawns)	1	0.41
E2EM1Pd	UPLAND	Residential (single family)	5	4.46
E2EM1Pd	UPLAND	Rangeland (shrub and brush cover) & Succession following ditching	1	1.91
E2EM1Pd	UPLAND	Transportation, Communications and Utilities	2	2.80
E2EM1Pd	UPLAND	Urban (golf courses)	1	0.32
Subtotal loss			**43**	**57.76**
E2EM1Ph	E1UBLh	Tidal restriction	2	5.51
E2EM1Ph	UPLAND	Commercial and Services (wharves, piers & shipyards)	1	1.16
E2EM1Ph	UPLAND	Forest (deciduous)	1	1.26
E2EM1Ph	UPLAND	Rangeland (shrub and brush cover)	2	1.74
Subtotal loss			**6**	**9.67**
E2EM1Phs	PEM1Rh	Tidal restriction & Succession	1	1.66
E2EM1Phs	PFO1R	Tidal restriction & Succession	1	0.41
E2EM1Phs	UPLAND	Rangeland (mixed), Tidal restriction & Succession	1	1.32
Subtotal loss			**3**	**3.39**

Code	Class	Description	Count	Value
E2EM1Ps	E2US2P	Coastal processes	1	1.31
E2EM1Ps	UPLAND	Barren Land (mixed barren land)	1	1.22
E2EM1Ps	UPLAND	Barren Land (sand areas other than Beaches)	1	0.67
E2EM1Ps	UPLAND	Commercial and Services (marinas)	1	1.44
E2EM1Ps	UPLAND	Rangeland (herbaceous cover)	1	7.77
E2EM1Ps	UPLAND	Rangeland (shrub and brush cover)	3	8.87
Subtotal loss			**8**	**21.27**
E2EM5P	PSS1R	Unknown	1	1.92
E2EM5P	PUBHh	Tidal restriction	1	0.43
E2EM5P	UPLAND	Rangeland (shrub and brush cover)	2	1.71
E2EM5P	UPLAND	Residential (lawns, includes non-residential lawns)	2	1.65
Subtotal loss			**5**	**3.79**
E2EM5P6h	UPLAND	Rangeland (shrub and brush cover)	1	0.72
E2EM5P6h	UPLAND	Residential (single family)	1	0.57
Subtotal loss			**2**	**1.29**
E2SS1P	UPLAND	Commercial and Services (commercial and institutional structures)	1	0.80
E2SS1P	UPLAND	Commercial and Services (paved surfaces)	1	0.87
E2SS1P	UPLAND	Commercial and Services (recreational structures)	1	0.33
E2SS1P	UPLAND	Rangeland (shrub and brush cover)	1	0.38
E2SS1P	UPLAND	Residential (single family)	1	0.54
Subtotal loss			**5**	**2.92**
E2SS1Pd	UPLAND	Agriculture (cropland)	1	0.55
E2SS1Pd	UPLAND	Forest (mixed)	1	1.63
E2SS1Pd	UPLAND	Industrial & Commercial Complexes	1	0.86
Subtotal loss			**3**	**3.04**
TOTAL LOSS OF VEGETATED COASTAL WETLAND			**314**	**361**

Gain in Vegetated Coastal Wetland

E1UBL6h	E2EM1/5P6h	Unknown	1	0.56
E2US4M6	E2EM1/5P6h	*P. australis* & *Typha angustifolia invasion*	1	0.83
PALUSTRINE FARMED	E2EM1/5P6h	Tidal restriction w/ *P. australis* invasion & Impoundment	1	0.44
U - Forest	E2EM1/5P6h	Succession following ditching & Impoundment	1	0.34
Subtotal gain			**4**	**2.17**
E1UBL	E2EM1N	Coastal processes	22	12.85
E2US2P	E2EM1N	Coastal processes	4	1.68
E2US2P	E2EM1N	Unknown	1	0.48
E2US2Ps	E2EM1N	Coastal processes	1	1.35
U - Rangeland	E2EM1N	Coastal processes	1	1.11
U - Forest	E2EM1N	Unknown	1	0.30
Subtotal gain			**30**	**17.76**
E1UBL	E2EM1P	Coastal processes	18	19.02
E1UBL	E2EM1P	Unknown	1	0.26
E1UBLx	E2EM1P	Excavation re-vegetated	2	1.27
E2US2M	E2EM1P	Coastal processes	2	0.55
E2US2N	E2EM1P	Coastal processes	1	3.93
E2US2P	E2EM1P	Coastal processes	3	2.54
E2US2Ps	E2EM1P	Coastal processes	1	1.86
E2US4M	E2EM1P	Coastal processes	5	12.06
E2US4Md	E2EM1P	Coastal processes & Succession following ditching	1	1.36
PUBHx	E2EM1P	Excavation, unknown use	1	1.06
U - Agriculture	E2EM1P	Coastal processes	1	3.77
U - Barren Land	E2EM1P	Unknown	1	3.21
U - Rangeland	E2EM1P	Coastal processes	1	0.44
Subtotal gain			**38**	**51.32**
E1UBL6	E2EM1P6	Coastal processes	2	0.94
E2US3M6	E2EM1P6	Coastal processes	1	0.26

E2US3M6	E2EM1P6	Unknown	1	0.66
U - Rangeland	E2EM1P6	Unknown	1	1.05
E1UBLh	E2EM1P6h	Tidal restriction	2	1.06
Subtotal gain			**5**	**2.91**
E1UBL	E2EM1Pd	Coastal processes & Succession following ditching	5	2.19
E2US2P	E2EM1Pd	Coastal processes & Succession following ditching	2	0.66
E2US2Ps	E2EM1Pd	Succession & Coastal processes	1	1.87
E2US3Md	E2EM1Pd	Succession following ditching & Coastal processes	1	3.28
E2US4Mx	E2EM1Pd	Unknown	1	0.61
U - Barren Land	E2EM1Pd	Succession following ditching	1	0.83
Subtotal gain			**11**	**9.43**
E1UBLh	E2EM1Ph	Succession	1	0.41
E1UBLh	E2EM1Ph	Tidal restriction	1	0.40
E1UBLh	E2EM1Ph	Unknown	1	2.42
U - Rangeland	E2EM1Ph	Tidal restriction & Coastal processes	1	1.00
Subtotal gain			**4**	**4.23**
E1UBL6	E2EM5/1P6	*P. australis and Typha angustifolia invasion*	2	1.76
Subtotal gain			**2**	**1.76**
E1UBL	E2EM5P	*Phragmites australis invasion*	2	0.82
E2US2N	E2EM5P	Coastal processes & Phragmites australis invasion	1	1.08
E2US2Ps	E2EM5P	Unknown	1	0.72
U - Commercial and Services	E2EM5P	Coastal processes & Phragmites australis invasion	1	0.37
U - Rangeland	E2EM5P	Coastal processes & Phragmites australis invasion	1	0.79
Subtotal gain			**6**	**3.79**
DUNE	E2EM5P6	Coastal processes & Phragmites australis invasion	1	0.33
E2US2N6hs	E2EM5P6	Tidal restriction & Succession	1	42.03
E2US2Ps	E2EM5P6	Succession & Phragmites australis invasion	1	0.53
Subtotal gain			**3**	**42.88**
E1UBL6h	E2EM5P6h	Tidal restriction w/ P. australis invasion	3	5.81
Palustrine farmed	E2EM5Pdh	Succession following ditching & Tidal restriction w/ P. australis invasion	2	2.68

			Count	Value
Subtotal gain			**5**	**8.49**
E1UBL6h		Tidal restriction w/ P. australis invasion	1	0.66
PFO1R		Impoundment & Phragmites australis invasion	1	0.96
Subtotal gain			**2**	**1.62**
E2US2P		Coastal processes	1	0.77
Subtotal gain			**1**	**0.77**
TOTAL GAIN OF COASTAL VEGETATED WETLAND			**111**	**147.11**

Change in Coastal Vegetated Type

			Count	Value
E2EM1/5P6	E2EM5/1P6	*Phragmites australis invasion*	1	5.28
E2EM1/5P6	E2EM5/1P6h	Unknown	1	1.21
E2EM1/5P6h	E2EM5P6h	Tidal restriction w/ P. australis invasion	1	0.81
E2EM1/5Pd	E2SS1Pd	Succession following ditching & Iva frutescens succession	1	5.11
E2EM1/5Pdh	E2EM5Pdh	Succession following ditching & Tidal restriction w/ P. australis invasion	1	4.25
Subtotal change in type			**5**	**16.66**
E2EM1N	E2EM1P	Unknown	10	15.72
E2EM1N	E2EM1Pd	Succession following ditching	3	3.34
E2EM1N	E2EM5P	*Phragmites australis invasion*	1	0.50
E2EM1N	E2SS1P	*Iva frutescens succession*	2	0.91
E2EM1N6	E2EM1/5P6h	Tidal restriction w/ P. australis invasion	1	1.53
E2EM1N6	E2EM5/1P6h	Tidal restriction w/ P. australis invasion	1	0.97
E2EM1Nd	E2EM1Pd	Succession following ditching	1	1.33
E2EM1Nh	E2EM1P6h	Tidal restriction	1	0.49
E2EM1Nh	E2EM1Ph	Tidal restriction	1	0.59
Subtotal change in type			**21**	**25.38**

From	To	Cause	n	Value
E2EM1P	E2EM1/SS1P	*Iva frutescens* succession	1	1.03
E2EM1P	E2EM1N	Unknown	6	1.54
E2EM1P	E2EM1Pd	Succession following ditching	1	1.04
E2EM1P	E2EM1Ph	Tidal restriction	1	0.23
E2EM1P	E2EM5/1P	*Phragmites australis* invasion	1	1.35
E2EM1P	E2EM5/1Pd	Succession following ditching & *Phragmites australis* invasion	1	0.71
E2EM1P	E2EM5P	*Phragmites australis* invasion	24	22.55
E2EM1P	E2EM5P	Unknown	1	0.89
E2EM1P	E2EM5P6	*Phragmites australis* invasion	1	3.19
E2EM1P	E2EM5P6d	Succession following ditching & *Phragmites australis* invasion	1	1.82
E2EM1P	E2EM5P6h	Tidal restriction w/ *P. australis* invasion	1	0.47
E2EM1P	E2EM5P6h	Unknown	1	0.39
E2EM1P	E2EM5Ph	Tidal restriction w/ *P. australis* invasion	1	0.57
E2EM1P	E2SS1P	*Iva frutescens* succession	14	13.54
Subtotal change in type			**55**	**49.34**
E2EM1P6	E2EM1/5P6	*P. australis* and *Typha angustifolia* invasion	1	1.17
E2EM1P6	E2EM1/5P6h	*P. australis* and *Typha angustifolia* invasion	6	18.29
E2EM1P6	E2EM5/1P6	*P. australis* and *Typha angustifolia* invasion	1	4.26
E2EM1P6	E2EM5/1P6h	*P. australis* and *Typha angustifolia* invasion	2	8.56
E2EM1P6	E2EM5P6	*Phragmites australis* invasion	3	2.20
E2EM1P6	E2EM5P6	Unknown	1	0.99
E2EM1P6	E2EM5P6h	Tidal restriction w/ *P. australis* invasion	2	0.81
E2EM1P6	E2EM5P6h	Succession following ditching & *Phragmites australis* invasion	1	1.36
E2EM1P6	E2EM5Pd	Succession following ditching & Tidal restriction w/ *P. australis* invasion	1	12.08
E2EM1P6d	E2EM1/5P6h	Succession following ditching	2	1.71
E2EM1P6d	E2EM5P6d	Succession following ditching & *Phragmites australis* invasion	1	1.32
E2EM1P6h	E2EM5P6h	Tidal restriction w/ *P. australis* invasion	2	1.04
Subtotal change in type			**23**	**53.77**
E2EM1Pd	E2EM1/5P6h	Tidal restriction w/ *P. australis* invasion	2	5.22
E2EM1Pd	E2EM1P	Succession following ditching	1	3.13
E2EM1Pd	E2EM1P6h	Tidal restriction	1	4.62
E2EM1Pd	E2EM1Ph	Tidal restriction	1	2.57

E2EM1Pd	E2EM5/1P6	*Phragmites australis* invasion	2	8.05
E2EM1Pd	E2EM5/1P6d	*Phragmites australis* invasion	1	4.39
E2EM1Pd	E2EM5P	Succession following ditching & Phragmites australis invasion	7	12.99
E2EM1Pd	E2EM5P	Unknown	1	0.56
E2EM1Pd	E2EM5P6	Unknown	1	4.10
E2EM1Pd	E2EM5P6d	*Phragmites australis* invasion	2	1.75
E2EM1Pd	E2EM5P6h	Succession following ditching & Tidal restriction w/ P. australis invasion	1	0.26
E2EM1Pd	E2EM5Pd	*Phragmites australis* invasion	9	9.31
E2EM1Pd	E2EM5Pd	Unknown	2	2.57
E2EM1Pd	E2EM5Pdh	Tidal restriction w/ P. australis invasion	5	12.80
E2EM1Pd	E2EM5Ph	Succession following ditching & Tidal restriction w/ P. australis invasion	2	1.39
E2EM1Pd	E2EM5Ph	Succession following ditching & Iva frutescens succession	9	16.34
E2EM1Pd	E2SS1P	Unknown	1	4.28
E2EM1Pd	E2SS1P	*Iva frutescens* succession	3	6.65
E2EM1Pd	E2SS1Pd	Tidal restriction & Iva frutescens succession	1	0.80
E2EM1Pd	E2SS1Ph	Succession following ditching	1	2.76
E2EM1Pdh	E2EM1Ph	Succession following ditching	1	0.78
E2EM1Pdh	E2EM5Ph	Succession following ditching & Tidal restriction w/ P. australis invasion	1	0.62
Subtotal change in type			**55**	**105.93**
E2EM1Ph	E2EM1P6	Tidal restriction	1	0.76
E2EM1Ph	E2EM1P6	Unknown	1	0.36
E2EM1Ph	E2EM5P6h	Tidal restriction w/ P. australis invasion	1	0.67
E2EM1Ph	E2EM5Ph	Tidal restriction w/ P. australis invasion	2	1.25
E2EM1Ph	E2EM5Ph	Unknown	1	0.78
E2EM1Ps	E2EM1P6h	Tidal restriction	1	14.27
E2EM1Ps	E2EM1Pd	Succession following ditching	1	3.62
E2EM1Ps	E2EM5P	*Phragmites australis* invasion	1	5.25
E2EM1Ps	E2EM5P6	Unknown	1	3.80
E2EM1Ps	E2SS1Pd	Succession following ditching & Iva frutescens succession	1	4.39
Subtotal change in type			**11**	**35.15**
E2EM5/1P6	E2EM1/5P6h	Tidal restriction w/ P. australis invasion	1	2.40
Subtotal change in type			**1**	**2.40**

From	To	Cause	Count	Area
E2EM5P	E2EM1N	Coastal processes	1	0.14
E2EM5P	E2EM5P6h	Tidal restriction w/ P. australis invasion	1	0.27
Subtotal change in type			**2**	**0.42**
E2EM5P6	E2EM1/5P6	*P. australis* and *Typha angustifolia* invasion	5	2.00
E2EM5P6	E2EM1/5P6h	*P. australis* and *Typha angustifolia* invasion	2	1.36
E2EM5P6	E2EM1/5P6h	Tidal restriction	1	1.80
E2EM5P6	E2EM1/5P6h	Unknown	1	1.01
Subtotal change in type			**9**	**6.16**
E2SS1P	E2EM1P	Unknown	2	2.28
E2SS1P	E2EM1Pdh	Succession following ditching & Tidal restriction	1	0.29
E2SS1P	E2EM5/1P	*P. australis* and *Typha angustifolia* invasion	1	3.30
E2SS1P	E2EM5P	*Phragmites australis* invasion	1	5.32
E2SS1P	E2EM5P6	*Phragmites australis* invasion	2	5.33
Subtotal change in type			**7**	**16.52**
E2SS1Pd	E2EM1Pd	Succession following ditching	1	7.23
E2SS1Pd	E2EM5P	Succession following ditching & *Phragmites australis* invasion	2	1.62
E2SS1Pd	E2EM5P6	Succession following ditching & *Phragmites australis* invasion	1	2.80
E2SS1Ph	E2EM1P6	Unknown	1	0.26
Subtotal change in type			**5**	**11.90**
TOTAL CHANGE IN VEGETATED COASTAL WETLAND TYPE			**194**	**323.64**

E2EM1/5P	1	1.63
E2EM1/5P6	1	0.50
E2EM1/5P6h	9	12.02
E2EM1/5Pdh	1	0.69
Subtotal no change	**12**	**14.84**
E2EM1/SS1P	2	2.63
E2EM1/SS1Pdh	1	3.23
Subtotal no change	**3**	**5.86**
E2EM1/US1N	2	2.37
E2EM1/US2P	1	0.27
E2EM1/US3N	3	3.43
Subtotal no change	**6**	**6.06**
E2EM1N	344	245.73
E2EM1N6	2	0.36
E2EM1N6h	1	0.45
E2EM1Nd	1	0.67
E2EM1Nh	8	6.22
Subtotal no change	**356**	**253.42**
E2EM1P	329	945.03
E2EM1P6	64	117.91
E2EM1P6d	3	9.03
E2EM1P6dh	1	3.10
E2EM1P6h	9	16.36
E2EM1Pd	85	1286.90

E2EM1Pdh	7	91.18
E2EM1Ph	16	25.81
Subtotal no change	**514**	**2495.32**
E2EM5/1P	3	6.97
E2EM5/1P6	5	19.35
E2EM5/SS1P	1	3.27
Subtotal no change	**9**	**29.59**
E2EM5P	62	105.74
E2EM5P5	16	30.46
E2EM5P6d	1	0.66
E2EM5P6dh	3	2.47
E2EM5P6h	15	27.62
E2EM5Pd	4	9.12
E2EM5Ph	2	8.47
Subtotal no change	**103**	**184.55**
E2SS1/EM1P	1	0.65
E2SS1P	77	89.53
E2SS1Pd	5	17.76
E2SS1Pdh	1	1.59
E2SS1Ph	1	0.34
Subtotal no change	**85**	**109.87**
TOTAL NO CHANGE IN VEGETATED COASTAL WETLAND	**1088**	**3099.50**

Table 5-A. Changes in nonvegetated coastal wetlands in the Narragansett Bay Estuary: 1950s to 1990s.

Type of Change	1950s Type	1990s Type	Cause of Change	Number of Sites	Acres
Loss of Nonvegetated Coastal Wetland					
	E2RF2N	E1UBL	Coastal processes	3	1.94
	Subtotal loss			**3**	**1.94**
	E2US2/EM1P	UPLAND	Residential (single family)	2	0.49
	Subtotal loss			**2**	**0.49**
	E2US2M	E1UBL	Coastal processes	4	62.33
	E2US2M	E2EM1P	Coastal processes	2	0.55
	E2US2Ms	E1UBL	Coastal processes	2	34.21
	Subtotal loss			**8**	**97.10**
	E2US2N	E1UBL	Coastal processes	13	42.45
	E2US2N	E1UBL	Unknown	1	0.58
	E2US2N	E2EM1P	Coastal processes	1	3.93
	E2US2N	E2EM5P	Coastal processes & Phragmites australis invasion	1	1.08
	E2US2N	UPLAND	Commercial and Services (paved surfaces)	1	0.49
	E2US2N	UPLAND	Residential (single family)	1	0.26
	Subtotal loss			**18**	**48.79**
	E2US2N6h	PUBHh	Unknown	1	0.97
	E2US2N6hs	E2EM5P6	Tidal restriction & Succession	1	42.03
	E2US2N6hs	UPLAND	Agriculture (pasture and hayfields)	1	7.92
	E2US2N6hs	UPLAND	Rangeland (shrub and brush cover)	1	3.42
	E2US2N6hs	UPLAND	Urban (golf courses)	4	27.77
	E2US2Ns	E1UBL	Unknown	1	0.88
	Subtotal loss			**9**	**82.98**

Code	Class	Cause	Count	Value
E2US2P	DUNE	Coastal processes	2	0.84
E2US2P	E1UBL	Coastal processes	19	16.87
E2US2P	E2EM1N	Coastal processes	4	1.68
E2US2P	E2EM1N	Unknown	1	0.48
E2US2P	E2EM1P	Coastal processes	3	2.54
E2US2P	E2EM1Pd	Coastal processes & Succession following ditching	2	0.66
E2US2P	E2SS1P	Coastal processes	1	0.77
E2US2P	PEM1Rh	Tidal restriction	1	1.68
E2US2P	UPLAND	Barren Land (mixed barren land)	2	2.71
E2US2P	UPLAND	Barren Land (sand areas other than Beaches)	1	1.29
E2US2P	UPLAND	Commercial and Services (marinas)	3	2.78
E2US2P	UPLAND	Rangeland (shrub and brush cover)	1	0.78
E2US2P	UPLAND	Residential (single family)	1	0.36
Subtotal loss			**41**	**33.42**
E2US2P6hs	PEM1R	Succession & Tidal restriction	1	1.42
E2US2P6hs	UPLAND	Rangeland (shrub and brush cover)	1	2.07
Subtotal loss			**2**	**3.49**
E2US2Ps	E1UBL	Coastal processes	4	9.81
E2US2Ps	E2EM1N	Coastal processes	1	1.35
E2US2Ps	E2EM1P	Coastal processes	1	1.86
E2US2Ps	E2EM1Pd	Coastal processes & Succession	1	1.86
E2US2Ps	E2EM5P	Unknown	1	0.72
E2US2Ps	E2EM5P6	Phragmites australis invasion	1	0.53
E2US2Ps	PEM5/SS1Rh	Succession & Tidal restriction w/ P. australis invasion	1	1.39
E2US2Ps	PEM5Rh	Succession & Tidal restriction w/ P. australis invasion	1	6.62
E2US2Ps	UPLAND	Barren Land (sand areas other than Beaches)	2	10.59
E2US2Ps	UPLAND	Commercial and Services (paved surfaces)	1	0.26
E2US2Ps	UPLAND	Forest (mixed)	2	1.00
E2US2Ps	UPLAND	Industrial	1	1.19
E2US2Ps	UPLAND	Rangeland (mixed)	5	24.17
E2US2Ps	UPLAND	Residential (single family)	3	1.59
E2US2Ps	UPLAND	Transportation, Communications and Utilities	3	6.73
E2US2Ps	UPLAND	Urban (golf courses)	1	6.64
E2US2Ps	UPLAND	Vegetation change, other	1	1.51

			Count	ha
Subtotal loss			**30**	**77.81**
E2US3M	E1UBL	Coastal processes	8	82.87
E2US3M	UPLAND	Commercial and Services (marinas)	1	1.25
E2US3M6	E2EM1P6	Coastal processes	1	0.26
E2US3M6	E2EM1P6	Unknown	1	0.66
E2US3Md	E2EM1Pd	Succession following ditching & Coastal processes	1	3.28
Subtotal loss			**12**	**88.32**
E2US4M	E2EM1P	Coastal processes	5	12.06
E2US4M6	E2EM1/5P6h	P. australis and Typha angustifolia invasion	1	0.83
E2US4Md	E2EM1P	Coastal processes & Succession following ditching	1	1.35
E2US4Ms	E1UBL	Coastal processes	1	0.26
E2US4Ms	PEM1R	Succession & Coastal processes	1	4.13
E2US4Mx	E2EM1Pd	Unknown	1	0.60
Subtotal loss			**10**	**19.24**
E2US4N	UPLAND	Barren Land (sand areas other than Beaches)	1	1.29
Subtotal loss			**1**	**1.29**
TOTAL LOSS OF NONVEGETATED COASTAL WETLAND			**136**	**454.86**

Gain of Nonvegetated Coastal Wetland

			Count	ha
E1UBL	E2RF2N	Oyster colonization	2	1.81
Subtotal gain			**2**	**1.81**
E1UBL	E2RS2Pr	Jetty/groin construction	2	0.52
Subtotal gain			**2**	**0.52**
DUNE	E2SB2N	Coastal processes	1	0.46
Subtotal gain			**1**	**0.46**
E2EM1P	E2SB3N	Coastal processes	1	0.54
Subtotal gain			**1**	**0.54**

From	To	Cause	Count	Area
E1UBL	E2US1N	Coastal processes	2	13.49
Subtotal gain			**2**	**13.49**
E1UBL	E2US1P	Coastal processes	2	4.19
E1UBL	E2US1P	Unknown	1	0.37
Subtotal gain			**3**	**4.55**
E2EM1P	E2US2/1N	Coastal processes	1	1.31
Subtotal gain			**1**	**1.31**
DUNE	E2US2M	Coastal processes	1	1.03
E1UBL	E2US2M	Coastal processes	8	15.79
E1UBL	E2US2M	Unknown	1	0.94
U - Commercial and Services	E2US2M		1	3.35
Subtotal gain			**11**	**21.11**
E1UBL	E2US2N	Coastal processes	22	17.49
E1UBL	E2US2N	Unknown	1	1.12
E2EM1P	E2US2N	Coastal processes	4	6.04
E2EM1P	E2US2Ns	Spoil deposition & Coastal processes	1	2.46
U - Agriculture	E2US2N	Coastal processes	1	0.72
U - Agriculture	E2US2Ns	Coastal processes & Spoil deposition	3	11.84
U - Barren Land	E2US2N	Coastal processes	1	3.42
U - Barren Land	E2US2Ns	Unknown	1	0.43
U - Commercial and Services	E2US2N	Coastal processes	1	0.45
U - Residential	E2US2N	Unknown	1	0.47
Subtotal gain			**36**	**44.43**
DUNE	E2US2P	Coastal processes	1	3.03
DUNE	E2US2P	Unknown	2	2.03
E1UBL	E2US2P	Coastal processes	30	27.43
E1UBL	E2US2P	Unknown	3	3.28
E2EM1N	E2US2P	Coastal processes	4	3.02
E2EM1N	E2US2P	Unknown	1	0.26

E2EM1P	E2US2P	Coastal processes	4	2.97
E2EM1P	E2US2P	Unknown	2	2.14
E2EM1P	E2US2P	*Phragmites australis* invasion	1	1.10
E2EM1Pd	E2US2P	Coastal processes	4	2.23
E2EM1Ps	E2US2P	Spoil deposition	1	1.31
E2RS2Pr	E2US2P	Jetty/groin removal	1	0.26
U - Barren Land	E2US2P	Coastal processes	2	2.94
U - Commercial and Services	E2US2P	Coastal processes	2	1.05
U - Commercial and Services	E2US2P	Structure removed	1	0.52
U - Rangeland	E2US2P	Coastal processes	2	0.59
U - Residential	E2US2P	Coastal processes	2	1.29
U - Trans., Communications and Utilities	E2US2P	Coastal processes	1	0.44
U - Unknown	E2US2P	Coastal processes	1	0.36
Subtotal gain			**65**	**56.23**
E1UBL	E2US3M	Coastal processes	11	31.67
E1UBL	E2US3M	Unknown	3	2.69
E2EM1N	E2US3M	Coastal processes	2	2.86
E2EM1P	E2US3M	Coastal processes	10	10.47
Subtotal gain			**26**	**47.68**
E1UBL	E2US3N	Coastal processes	16	31.89
E1UBL	E2US3N6h	Tidal restriction	2	0.51
E1UBL	E2US3Nh	Tidal restriction	4	3.41
E1UBL6	E2US3N6	Coastal processes	3	1.30
E1UBL6	E2US3N6h	Tidal restriction	2	1.72
E1UBL6	E2US3N6h	Unknown	1	1.24
E2EM1N	E2US3N	Unknown	1	0.37
E2RF2N	E2US3N	Coastal processes	3	1.24
Subtotal gain			**32**	**41.68**
E2EM1P6	E2US4M	Unknown	1	1.41
Subtotal gain			**1**	**1.41**

From type	To type	Cause	Count	Value
M1UBL	M2RS2Pr	Jetty/groin construction	1	0.71
Subtotal gain			**1**	**0.71**
E1UBL6	M2US2P	Coastal processes	1	0.41
Subtotal gain			**1**	**0.41**
TOTAL GAIN OF NONVEGETATED COASTAL WETLAND			**184**	**235.80**

Change in Nonvegetated Coastal Type

From type	To type	Cause	Count	Value
E2US2M	E2US2N	Coastal processes	2	1.25
E2US2M	E2US2P	Coastal processes	3	2.22
E2US2M	E2US3N	Coastal processes	1	0.77
E2US2Ms	E2US2P	Coastal processes	1	0.94
Subtotal change in type			**7**	**5.18**
E2US2N	E2US2M	Coastal processes	1	0.63
E2US2N	E2US2P	Coastal processes	3	1.74
E2US2N	E2US3M	Coastal processes	1	1.12
E2US2N	E2US3M	Unknown	1	12.44
Subtotal change in type			**6**	**15.93**
E2US2P	E2US2/1N	Coastal processes	1	1.61
E2US2P	E2US2M	Coastal processes	2	1.78
E2US2P	E2US2N	Coastal processes	14	13.51
E2US2P	E2US2N	Unknown	2	0.72
E2US2P	E2US3M	Coastal processes	2	1.27
E2US2P	E2US4N	Coastal processes	1	0.08
E2US2Ps	E2US2N	Coastal processes	3	4.43
E2US2Ps	E2US2P	Spoil deposition	3	3.54
Subtotal change in type			**28**	**26.93**
E2US3M	E2US2P	Coastal processes	1	0.54
Subtotal change in type			**1**	**0.54**

	Coastal processes	
M2US2P	2	5.97
Subtotal change in type	**2**	**5.97**
TOTAL CHANGE IN NONVEGETATED WETLAND TYPE	**44**	**55.00**

No Change in Nonvegetated Coastal Wetland

E2RF2N	2	4.33
E2RF2Nh	3	3.17
Subtotal no change	**5**	**7.50**
E2RS1N	29	29.15
Subtotal no change	**29**	**29.15**
E2RS1P	54	97.12
Subtotal no change	**54**	**97.12**
E2RS2N	38	75.60
E2RS2Nr	4	1.13
Subtotal no change	**42**	**76.73**
E2RS2P	7	12.64
E2RS2Pr	12	2.98
Subtotal no change	**19**	**15.62**
E2SB2N	1	0.17
E2SB3N	2	1.87
Subtotal no change	**3**	**2.04**
E2US1/2N	1	2.75
E2US1N	25	52.07
Subtotal no change	**26**	**54.82**

Code	Count	Value
E2US1P	15	55.15
Subtotal no change	**15**	**55.15**
E2US2/1N	16	39.29
E2US2/EM1N	2	5.94
Subtotal no change	**18**	**45.23**
E2US2M	18	231.31
Subtotal no change	**18**	**231.31**
E2US2N	240	380.02
Subtotal no change	**240**	**380.02**
E2US2P	225	515.62
Subtotal no change	**225**	**515.62**
E2US3M	35	138.24
Subtotal no change	**35**	**138.24**
E2US3N	45	65.23
E2US3N6	1	0.59
E2US3N6h	2	1.66
E2US3Nd	1	2.76
Subtotal no change	**49**	**70.24**
E2US4M	23	36.64
E2US4Md	2	0.93
E2US4Mh	1	0.61
Subtotal no change	**26**	**38.19**
E2US4N	2	1.64
Subtotal no change	**2**	**1.64**
M2RS1N	73	122.92
Subtotal no change	**73**	**122.92**
M2RS1P	76	192.96

Subtotal no change	76	192.96
M2RS2N	12	19.40
M2RS2Nr	1	0.41
Subtotal no change	13	**19.81**
M2RS2P	3	8.90
Subtotal no change	3	**8.90**
M2US1N	2	5.91
Subtotal no change	2	**5.90**
M2US1P	4	9.57
Subtotal no change	4	**9.57**
M2US2M	1	2.28
Subtotal no change	1	**2.28**
M2US2N	14	94.92
Subtotal no change	14	**9.00**
M2US2P	14	76.96
Subtotal no change	14	**76.96**
TOTAL NO CHANGE IN NONVEGETATED COASTAL WETLAND	1006	**2206.90**

Appendix B. Summary Tables for Individual Study Areas

Table 1-B.   Trends in estuarine wetlands for Allins Cove from the 1930s to the 1950s and from the 1950s to the 1990s.

Table 2-B.   Trends in estuarine wetlands for Calf Pasture Point from the 1930s to the 1950s and from the 1950s to the 1990s.

Table 3-B.   Trends in estuarine wetlands for Jacobs Point from the 1930s to the 1950s and from the 1950s to the 1990s.

Table 4-B.   Trends in estuarine wetlands for Palmer River from the 1930s to the 1950s and from the 1950s to the 1990s.

Table 5-B.   Trends in estuarine wetlands for Sachuest Point from the 1930s to the 1950s and from the 1950s to the 1990s.

Table 6-B.   Trends in estuarine wetlands for Wesquage Pond from the 1930s to the 1950s and from the 1950s to the 1990s.

Table 1-B. Trends in estuarine wetlands for Allins Cove from the 1930s to the 1950s and from the 1950s to the 1990s (excluding type changes within the wetland class).

Wetland Type* Change /Cause	1930-50 Acres Changed	Change/Cause	1950-90 Acres Changed**
Unconsolidated Shore			
EEM/Coastal Processes	-1.6	EWH/Coastal Processes	-0.6
Dune/Coastal Processes	-1.2	U/Residential (lawn)	-0.4
EWH/Coastal Processes	+0.4	EWH/Coastal Processes	+0.8
Dune/Coastal Processes	+0.3	EEM/Coastal Processes	+1.5
EWH/Coastal Processes			+10.9
EWH/Unknown			+0.6
EEM/Coastal Processes			+2.1
Net Change	-2.1		+14.9
Emergent Wetland	-3.7	EWH/Coastal Processes	-2.1
EUS/Coastal Processes			
EWH/Unknown	-0.3	EUS/Coastal Processes	-0.6
Dune/Coastal Processes	-6.9	U/Golf course	-0.6
U/Residential (single-family)	+0.4	EWH/Unknown	-3.2
U/Golf course	+0.2	EWH/Coastal Processes	-3.4
ESS/Ditching	+0.4	ESS/Unknown	-5.5
PEM/Tidal Restriction/Ditching	+0.3	ESS/Phragmites invasion	-4.3
EWH/Coastal Processes			+3.3
EUS/Coastal Processes			+0.6
Dune/Coastal Processes			+0.3
Net Change	-9.6		-15.5
Scrub-Shrub Wetland	-0.4	EEM/Unknown	+5.5
EEM/Ditching			
	-0.3	EEM/Phragmites invasion	
Net Change	-0.7		+5.5
NET CHANGE ALL	-12.4		+4.9

Table 2-B. Trends in estuarine wetlands for Calf Pasture Point from the 1930s to the 1950s and from the 1950s to the 1990s (excluding type changes within the wetland class).

Wetland Type* Change/Cause	1930-50 Acres Changed	Change/Cause	1950-90 Acres Changed**	
Unconsolidated Shore EWH/Coastal Processes	-2.7	EWH/Coastal Processes	-51.5	
EEM/Coastal Processes	-4.4	U/Barren Land (mixed)	-7.1	
EEM/Coastal Process/Ditching	-9.9	U/Commercial&Services	-1.4	
U/Rangeland	+13.0	EWH/Coastal Processes	-25.7	
EWH/Coastal Processes	+52.8	EWH/Spoil Deposition	+2.4	
EEM/Spoil Deposition	+2.2	EEM/Coastal Processes	+1.3	
U/Coastal Processes	+6.5	EEM/Spoil Deposition	+2.5	
ERS/Jetty-groin Removal			+0.3	
Net Change	*+57.5*		*-79.2*	
Emergent Wetland Dune/Coastal Processes	-1.6	EWH/Coastal Processes	-0.9	
EWH/Coastal Processes	-1.7	EWH/Tidal Restriction	-2.8	
PEM/Phragmites invasion	-2.2	EUS/Coastal Processes	-6.6	
EUS/Spoil Deposition	-6.5	EUS/Spoil Deposition	-1.3	
U/Rangeland	-0.8	U/Agriculture (hay/pasture)	-1.2	
(landfill)	-33.9	U/Barren Land (mixed)	-1.6	U/Urban
(mixed)	-3.8	U/Commercial&Services	-2.4	U/Forest
Course	-9.0	U/Rangeland (mixed)	-0.2	U/Golf
PSS/Spoil Deposition	-1.5	U/Transp., Commun, & Util.	-5.6	
PSS/Unknown	-4.0	U/Ditching	-1.9	
ESS/Ditching	+3.3	EWH/Coastal Processes	-4.4	
EUS/Coastal Processes	+0.4	EWH/Unknown	+8.4	
	+0.3	EWH/Phragmites		

	Net Change	-61.1		-20.4
Scrub-Shrub		-5.2	U/Barren Land (mixed)	+4.4
EEM/Ditching				

| NET CHANGE ALL | -8.7 | | -95.2 |

*EWH = estuarine deepwater habitat; EUS = Estuarine Unconsolidated Shore; EEM = Estuarine Emergent Wetland; ESS = Estuarine Scrub-Shrub Wetland; ERS = Estuarine Rocky Shore; PEM = Palustrine Emergent Wetland; PSS = Palustrine Scrub-Shrub Wetland; U = Upland.

**For losses (-) habitat designated is type changed to, whereas for gains (+) habitat designated is the former habitat.

Table 3-B. Trends in estuarine wetlands for Jacobs Point from the 1930s to the 1950s and from the 1950s to the 1990s (excluding type changes within the wetland class).

Wetland Type* Change/Cause	1930-50 Acres Changed	Change/Cause	1950-90 Acres Changed**
Unconsolidated Shore	0	na	+1.4
EUS/Coastal Processes			
			+0.6
EWH/Coastal Processes			
Net Change	*0*		*+2.0*
Emergent Wetland	-2.6	U/Agriculture	-2.0
U/Rangeland			
			-0.4
U/Residential (lawn)			
			-1.4
EUS/Coastal Processes			
			-1.8
ESS/Ditching			
			+10.0
ESS/Ditching			
			+2.7
ESS/Phragmites invasion			
Net Change	*-2.6*		*+7.1*
Scrub-Shrub Wetland	0	na	-10.0
EEM/Ditching			
			-2.7
EEM/Phragmites invasion			
			+1.8
EEM/Ditching			
Net Change	*0*		*-10.9*
NET CHANGE ALL	*-2.6*		*-1.8*

*EWH = estuarine deepwater habitat; EUS = Estuarine Unconsolidated Shore; EEM = Estuarine Emergent Wetland; ESS = Estuarine Scrub-Shrub Wetland; U = Upland; na - not applicable.
** Note: For losses (-) habitat designated is type changed to, whereas for gains (+) habitat designated is the former habitat (i.e., changed from).

Table 4-B. Trends in estuarine wetlands for the Palmer River System from the 1930s to the 1950s and from the 1950s to the 1990s (excluding type changes within the wetland class).

Wetland Type* Change/Cause	1930-50 Acres Changed	Change/Cause	1950-90 Acres Changed**
Unconsolidated Shore EEM/Unknown	+0.6	U-Barren Land/Unknown	-0.6
			+0.5 EWH/Unknown +1.7
EWH/Coastal Processes			
Net Change	*+0.6*		*+1.6*
Emergent Wetland U/Residential (single-family)	-0.5	EWH/Coastal Processes	-1.9
U/Residential Lawn	-0.6	U/Barren Land (mixed)	-0.4
U/Commercial&Services	-0.4	U/Residential (single-family)	-0.6
ESS/Succession	-0.7	U/Commercial&Services	-1.1
ESS/Phragmites-Ditching	-1.2	PEM/Tidal Restriction	+6.9
EWH/Coastal Processes			+1.4
EWH/Coastal Processes-Ditching			+0.9
EUS/Unknown			+0.6
U/Barren Land-Spoil-Ditching			+0.8
Net Change	*-3.4*		*+6.6*
Scrub-Shrub Wetland U/Rangeland	0	N/A	-0.4
EEM/Phragmites-Ditching			-6.9
EEM/Succession			+1.1
Net Change	*0*		*-6.2*
NET CHANGE ALL	*-2.8*		*+2.0*

* EWH =estuarine deepwater habitat; EUS = Estuarine Unconsolidated Shore; EEM = Estuarine Emergent Wetland; ESS = Estuarine Scrub-Shrub Wetland; U = Upland.
** Note: For losses (-) habitat designated is type changed to, whereas for gains (+) habitat designated is the former habitat (i.e., changed from).

Table 5-B. Trends in estuarine wetlands for Sachuest Point from the 1930s to the 1950s and from the 1950s to the 1990s (excluding type changes within the wetland class).

Wetland Type* Change/Cause	1930-50 Acres Changed	Change/Cause	1950-90 Acres Changed**
Unconsolidated Shore	-3.2	EEM/Coastal Processes	+1.0
U-Residential/Coastal Processes			
	-2.5	EEM/Phragmites invasion	+1.3
U-Recreation/Coastal Process&			
	-0.5	U/Commercial&Services	
Structure Removal			
			+0.5
EWH/Coastal Processes			
Net Change	*-6.2*		*+2.8*
Emergent Wetland	-1.2	U/Residential (lawn)	-4.4
Commercial&Services			
	-1.2	U/Residential (single-family)	-9.0
Rangeland (herbaceous)			
	-1.0	U/Commercial&Services	-12.3
Rangeland (shrub)			
	-1.4	U/Transp., Commun.,& Utili.	-0.7
Barren Land (sand)			
	+3.2	EUS/Coastal Processes	+1.0
EWH/Unknown			
	+2.5	EUS/Phragmites invasion	
	+5.3	ESS/Spoil Deposition	
Net Change	*+6.2*		*-25.4*
Scrub-Shrub Wetland	-5.3	EEM/Spoil Deposition	0
Net Change	*-5.3*		*0*
NET CHANGE ALL	*-5.3*		*-22.6*

* EWH = estuarine deepwater habitat; EUS = Estuarine Unconsolidated Shore; EEM = Estuarine Emergent Wetland; ESS = Estuarine Scrub-Shrub Wetland U = Upland.
** <u>Note</u>: For losses (-) habitat designated is type changed to, whereas for gains (+) habitat designated is the former habitat.

Table 6-B. Trends in estuarine wetlands for Wesquage Pond from the 1930s to the 1950s and from the 1950s to the 1990s (excluding type changes within the wetland class).

Wetland Type* Change/Cause	1930-50 Acres Changed	Change/Cause	1950-90 Acres Changed**
Streambed	0	na	+0.5
Dune/Coastal Processes			
Net Change	*0*		*+0.5*
Rocky Shore	0	na	+0.3
EWH/Jetty-groin Construction			
Net Change	*0*		*+0.3*
Unconsolidated Shore	-47.6	EWH/Tidal Restriction	-1.1
U/Residential (single-family)			
	-0.8	EEM/Tidal Restriction	
	-0.5	Dune/Coastal Processes	
	-0.3	ESS/Tidal Restriction	
	+0.3	EWH/Coastal Processes	
Net Change	*-48.9*		*-1.1*
Emergent Wetland	+0.2	EWH/Tidal Restriction	-4.4
EWH/Tidal Restriction			
	+0.8	EUS/Tidal Restriction	-2.7
U/Commercial&Services (paved)			
			-0.6
U/Residential (single-family)			
			-1.5
U/Rangeland (shrub)			
			+0.6
EWH/Unknown			
			+0.8
EWH/Tidal Restriction			
			+3.6
EWH/Tidal Restriction-Phragmites			
			+0.3
ESS/Unknown			
Net Change	*+1.0*		*-3.9*
Scrub-Shrub Wetland	-0.4	U/Commercial&Services	-0.3
EEM/Unknown			
	+0.3	EUS/Tidal Restriction	
Net Change	*-0.1*		*-0.3*
NET CHANGE ALL	*-48.0*		*-4.5*

* EWH = estuarine deepwater habitat; EUS = Estuarine Unconsolidated Shore; EEM = Estuarine Emergent Wetland; U = Upland; na - not applicable.
** Note: For losses (-) habitat designated is type changed to, whereas for gains (+) habitat designated is the former habitat.